Walks in London Borough Haringey

by
John N. Merrill

Maps, pencil sketches, Chinese Brush paintings and photographs by John N. Merrill

"I hike the paths and trails of the world for others to enjoy."

THE JOHN MERRILL FOUNDATION

The London Borough Walks Series - Vol Three.

2008

THE JOHN MERRILL FOUNDATION
32, Holmesdale, Waltham Cross, Hertfordshire, England. EN8 8QY

Tel/Fax - 01992-762776
E-mail - marathonhiker@aol.com
www. johnmerrillwalkguides.com
WWW.walkinglondon.org

A catalogue record for this book is available from the British Library.

Typset and designed by *The John Merrill Foundation*
Printed and handmade by *John N. Merrill.*
Book layout and cover design by *John N. Merrill*

©Text and photograpghs - by John N. Merrill, HonMUniv, 2008.
© Maps, sketches & paintings, by John N. Merrill, HonMUniv, 2008.
ISBN 978 -0-9556511-8-2
First published - July 2008.
Special limited edition.

Typeset in Humanst521 - bold, italic, and plain 11pt, 14pt and 18pt Main titles in 18pt .**Humanst521 Bd BT** by John Merrill in Adobe Pagemaker on a iMac.

Please note - *The maps in this guide are purely illustrative. You are encouraged to use the appropriate 1:25,000 O.S. Explorer map as detailed on each walk.*

John Merrill confirms he has walked all the routes in this book and detailed what he found. Meticulous research has been undertaken to ensure that this publication is highly accurate at the time of going to press. The publishers, however, cannot be held responsible for alterations, errors, omissions, or for changes in details given. They would welcome information to help keep the book up to date.

Cover photograph - London skyline view from Alexandra Palace
   - by John N. Merrill

A little about John N. Merrill

Few people have walked the earth's crust more than John Merrill with more than 183,000 miles (36,600,000 strides) in the last 35 years - the average person walks 75,000 miles in a lifetime. Apart from walking too much causing bones in his feet to snap, like metal fatigue, he has never suffered from any back, hip or knee problems. Like other walkers he has suffered from many blisters, his record is 23 on both feet! He wears out at least three pairs of boots a year and his major walking has cost over £135,000. This includes over 103 pairs of boots costing more than £12,000, 43 rucksacks, £3,500 and over £2,000 on socks - a pair of socks last three weeks and don't have time to be washed!

His marathon walks in Britain include -

Hebridean Journey....... 1,003 miles. Northern Isles Journey......913 miles.
Irish Island Journey ....1,578 miles.   Parkland Journey.......2,043 miles.
Land's End to John o' Groats.....1,608 miles.
The East of England Heritage Route - 450miles.

and in 1978 he became the first person to walk the entire coastline of Britain - 6,824 miles in ten months.

In Europe he has walked across Austria - 712 miles - hiked the Tour of Mont Blanc, the Normandy coast, the Loire Valley (450 miles), a high level route across the Augverne(230 miles) and the River Seine (200 miles) in France, completed High Level Routes in the Dolomites and Italian Alps, and the GR20 route across Corsica in training! Climbed the Tatra Mountains ,the Transylvanian Alps in Romania, and in Germany walked in the Taunus, Rhine, the Black Forest (Clock Carriers Way) and King Ludwig Way (Bavaria). He has walked across Europe - 2,806 miles in 107 days - crossing seven countries, the Swiss and French Alps and the complete Pyrennean chain - the hardest and longest mountain walk in Europe, with more than 600,000 feet of ascent! In 1998 he walked 1,100 miles along the pilgrimage route from Le Puy (France) to Santiago (Spain) and onto Cape Finisterre; in 2002 walked 700 miles from Seville to Santiago de Compostela. In 2003 he walked 650 miles through the length of Portual via Fatima to Santiago de Compostela (Spian), pioneering a "lost" medieval route; 400 miles from Oslo to Trondheim, following St. Olav's Way, and all the trails on the Hong Kong Islands.

In America he used The Appalachian Trail - 2,200 miles - as a training walk, before walking from Mexico to Canada via the Pacific Crest Trail in record time - 118 days for 2,700 miles. Recently he walked most of the Continental Divide Trail and much of New Mexico; his second home. In 1999 he walked the Chesopeake &

The author with his medal after taking part in the 2008 Walk for Life Charity walk.

Ohio Canal National Historical Trail. In 2,000 he became the first thru hiker to walk 1,340 miles around Ohio, following the Buckeye Trail. In Canada he has walked the Rideau Trail - Kingston to Ottowa - 220 miles and The Bruce Trail - Tobermory to Niagara Falls - 460 miles.

In 1984 John set off from Virginia Beach on the Atlantic coast, and walked 4,226 miles without a rest day, across the width of America to Santa Cruz and San Francisco on the Pacific coast. This is one of the finest and most memorable walks, being in modern history, the longest, hardest crossing of the U.S.A. in the shortest time - under six months (178 days). The direct distance is 2,800 miles.

He has walked all of our National Trails many times - The Cleveland Way thirteen times and The Pennine Way four times in a year! He has been trekking in the Himalayas five times. He created more than forty challenge walks which have been used to raise more than £752,200 for various charities. From his own walks he has raised over £151,000. He is author of more than 300 walking guides and more than 100 other books by other authors, which he prints and publishes himself. His book sales are in excess of 3 3/4 million. He has created many long distance walks including The Limey Way, The Peakland Way, Dark Peak Challenge walk, Rivers' Way, The Belvoir Witches Challenge Walk, The Forest of Bowland Challenge, the Lincolnshire Wolds "Black Death" Challenge Walk and the Happy Hiker (White Peak) Challenge Walk, Jennifer's Challenge Walk and The Epping Forest Challenge Walk. His new Pilgrim Walk Series includes the 36 mile, "Walsingham Way" - King's Lynn to Walsingham, St. Winefride's Way in Flintshire and St. Albans Way in Hertfordshire. He is currently writing a series of books about walks in the London area , including - "Walking the Streets of London" , "Walking the Canals of London", "The Big Walks of London", & "Guides to every London Borough", so far he has walked over 2,800 miles, including the Capital Ring, London Loop, River Lee Navigation, Jubilee Way, Wandle Trail, and the Pymmes Brook Trail. In January 2003, he was honoured for his walking and writing, recieving a Honorary degree, Master of the University, from Derby University. In 2006 he was made Honorary member of The Paxton Society, for his book on *Sir Joseph Paxton*. He lectures extensively about his walking.

4

CONTENTS

INTRODUCTION

Before I started this book I was familiar with the Capital Ring, New River and River Lee Navigation that passes through the borough; but the rest was unknown. First I ventured to Alexandra's Palace and Park to explore and see the views to London's skyline. A few days later I set off from Bruce's Castle to begin walking the twelve mile "Better Haringey" walk, which is basically a borough boundary walk of great diversity. I hadn't gone more than a dozen strides, when a local asked, *"Where I was walking to"*? *"Right round the borough"*, I replied. *"There's nothing of interest in Haringey"*, she said. We said good-bye and off I walked to discover Haringey for myself.

She was wrong, for as I walked and explored I found much of interest - buildings, excellent parks, woods and fascinating history. With that walk behind me I continued exploring other parts of the borough; every walk became absorbing. Although I had walked through Tottenham Marshes, I never knew of the gruesome story of the Tottenham Outrage. Tottenham itself became a surprise with many fascinating buildings, with the High Cross and well, around the original village.

Another walk from Tottenham enabled me to link six parks together in one circular walk and proved stunning, especially Downhills Park. Finsbury Park I linked with the New River but came back to do more walks here, for it is without doubt one of the finest parks in North London. One such walk took me from the park to Crouch End and its historic Clock Tower, before discovering Priory Park and the small, but stunning, Stationers Park.

Tucked away are several woods and "hidden" parks and other shorter walks brought me to these, including Coldfall Wood, Bluebell Wood, the Railway Fields Nature Reserve and Woodside Park.

Haringey has much to offer the walker and deserves to be better known. These walks combined cover the whole borough and bring you to every park, historic building and peaceful river and navigation. Take the bus or underground to a walks' start and see for yourself the history and scenic parks on your doorstep. For me, I continue my journey, and cross the River Lee Navigation and begin walking and exploring Waltham Forest; as one walk book ends another starts!

Happy walking! John N. Merrill

The Art of Walking the John Merrill Way.

1. Always set off in the clothes you plan to wear all day, given the weather conditions. Only on sudden changes in the weather will I stop and put on a waterproof or warmer clothing.

2. Set off at a steady comfortable pace, which you can maintain all day. You should end the walk as fresh as when as you started.

3. Maintain your pace and don't stop. Stopping for any period of time disrupts your rhythm and takes upwards of a mile to settle back down into the flow/ease of movement.

4. Switch off your mobile phone and music centre, and listen and enjoy the countryside - the smells of the flowers, bird song, the rustle of the leaves and the tinkling stream.

5. Ignore the mileage and ascents - don't tick off the miles, just concentrate on what the walk's goal is. To think otherwise slows you down and makes the walk a struggle rather than a joy. In a similar vein, when ascending just keep a steady pace and keep going. To stop is to disrupt the flow and make the ascent interminable.

6. Whilst a walk is a challenge to complete, it is not just exercise. You should enjoy the world around you; the flowers, birds, wildlife and nature and look at and explore the historical buildings and church's that you pass. All are part of life's rich tapestry.

7. Remember that for every mile that you walk, you extend your life by 21 minutes.

8. A journey of a 1,000 miles begins with a single step and a mile requires 2,000 strides.

*"The expert traveller
leaves no footprints."*
Lao Tzu.

HOW TO DO A WALK

Every walk in this book follows a public right of way, be it a footpath, bridleway, Boat or RUPP, which are marked in green lines on the Ordnance Survey 1:25,000 Explorer maps.

On each walk I have detailed which map is needed and I would urge you to carry and use the map. As I walk I always have the map out on the section I am walking, constantly checking that I am walking the right way. Also when coming to any road or path junction, I can check on the map to ensure I take the right route.

Most the paths are signed and waymarked with coloured arrows but I would at best describe them as intermittent. They act as confirmation of the right of way you are walking and the arrow points in the direction of travel.

The countryside has the added problem of vandalism and you will find path logo's and Information Boards spray painted over and path signs pointing the wrong way! That is why I always advise carrying the map open on the area you are walking to check you are walking the right way. In my walking instructions I have given the name of each main and minor road, canal lock, and bridge, together with the house numbers where you turn and the name of inns passed. All to help you have a smooth and trouble free walk.

I confirm I have walked every route and written what I found at the time of walking.

These comments are not meant to put you off but to make you aware of some of the problems of walking in the countryside.

ABOUT THE WALKS
- some general comments.

Whilst every care is taken detailing and describing the walks in this book, it should be borne in mind that the countryside changes by the seasons and the work of man. I have described the walk to the best of my ability, detailing what I have found actually on the walk in the way of stiles and signs. You should always walk with the appropriate O.S. map, as detailed for each walk, open on the walk area for constant reference. Obviously with the passage of time stiles become broken or replaced by a ladder stile, a small gate or a kissing gate. Signs too have a habit of being broken or pushed over - vandelism. All the route follow rights of way and only on rare occasions will you have to overcome obstacles in its path, such as a blown down tree, barbed wire fence or an electric fence. On rare occasions rights of way are rerouted and these ammendments are included in the next edition. Inns have a frustrating habit of changing their name, then back to the original one!

All rights of way have colour coded arrows; on marker posts, stiles/gates and trees; these help you to show the direction of the right of way -

Yellow - Public footpath.
Blue - Public bridleway.
Red - Byway open to all traffic (BOAT).
Black - Road used as a public path (RUPP).
White - Concessionary and Permissive path

The seasons bring occasional problems whilst out walking which should also be borne in mind. In the height of summer paths become overgrown and you may have to fight your way through in a few places. In low lying areas the fields are often full of crops, and although the pathline goes straight across it may be more practical to walk round the field edge to get to the next stile or gate. In summer the ground is generally dry but in autumn and winter, especially because of our climate, the surface can be decidedly wet and slippery; sometimes even gluttonous mud!

These comments are part of countryside walking which help to make your walk more interesting or briefly frustrating. Standing in a track up to your ankles in mud might not be funny at the time but upon reflection was one of the highlights of the walk!

The mileage for each section is based on three calculations -

1. pedometer and stepometer readings.
2. the route map measured on the map.
3. the time I took for the walk.

I believe the figure stated for each section to be very accurate but we all walk differently and not always in a straight line! The time allowed for each section is on the generous side and does not include pub stops etc. The figure is based on the fact that on average a person walks 2 1/2 miles an hours but less in hilly terrain. Allow 20 minutes to walk a mile; ten minutes for 1/2 mile and five minutes for 1/4 mile. On average you will walk 2,000 strides to a mile - an average stride is 31 inches..

"For every mile you walk, you extend your life by 21 minutes"

Follow the Countryside Code.

* Be safe - plan ahead
and follow any signs.

* Leave gates and property
as you find them.

* Protect plants and animals, and take
your litter home.

* Keep dogs
under close control.

* Consider
other people.

THE CAPITAL RING IN HARINGEY - 4 1/2 MILES

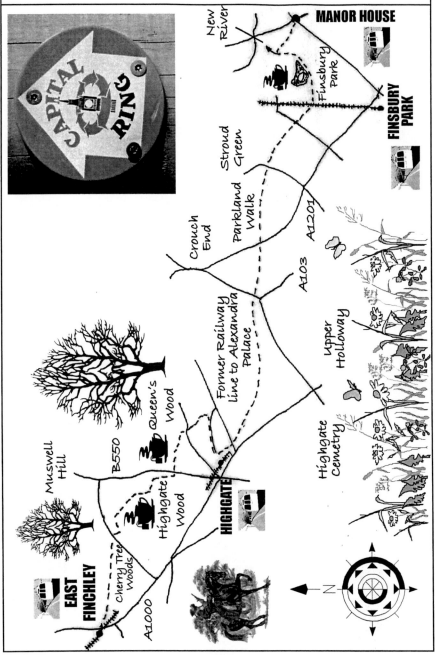

CAPITAL RING

MANOR HOUSE

New River

Finsbury Park

FINSBURY PARK

Stroud Green

Parkland Walk

Crouch End

A1201

A103

Upper Holloway

Former Railway Line to Alexandra Palace

Highgate Cemetery

Queen's Wood

Muswell Hill

B550

Highgate Wood

HIGHGATE

Cherry Tree Woods

EAST FINCHLEY

A1000

N

THE CAPITAL RING IN HARINGEY
- 4 1/2 MILES
- allow 2 hours

Basic route - East Finchley Underwood Station - Cherry Tree Woods - Lancaster Road - Bridge Gate - Highgate Wood - Queens Wood - Highgate Underground Station - Former Alexandra Palace Railway Line (Parkland Walk) - Finsbury Park - Manor House Underground Station.

Map - O.S. 1:25,000 Explorer Series No. 173 - London North. - Capital Ring leaflets - Walks 11 and 12.

Start - East Finchley Underground Station (Northern Line - High Barnet branch).
Bus nos. 143, 234, & 263.

End - Manor House Underground Station (Piccadilly Line).
Bus nos. 29, 253, 254, 259.
Less than half way you pass Highgate Underground Station (Northern Line - High Barnet Branch).

Inns - at the start in East Finchley and end at Manor House.

Cafe's - Park Cafe's in Cherry Tree Woods - The Lazy Sally; Highgate Woods, just off the route and in Finsbury Park.

ABOUT THE WALK - One of the most enjoyable sections of the Capital Ring lies in Haringey. The route takes you first through a park before the woodland of Highgate Wood and Queens Wood. Next you have a two mile level stretch along a former railway line - Parkland Walk - to Finsbury Park; a premier open space in North London.

In the northern corner of the park is the New River - the next walk. These two walks can be joined together to make a fine 9 mile walk, which could be made into a circular of walk of 12 miles, by walking through Alexandra Palace Park - see separate section.

WALKING INSTRUCTIONS - Starting from East Finchley Station (High Street entrance), cross the main road and turn right before the railway bridge into Brompton Grove. In a short distance turn right onto the tarmaced path and into Cherry Tree Woods Park & Recreation grounds. Keep straight ahead along its lefthand side, past the Children's Play Area, cafe - Lazy Sally - and Tennis courts to Fordington Road. Keep straight ahead along the road to the road junction. Cross into Lancaster Road and before the road turns right, turn left at house no. 69, and walk up the tarmaced drive to Highgate Wood. In the late stages the path bears right to the Bridge Gate entrance. Walk through the ornate "nature gates".

Keep straight ahead along the wide path through the woods to a drinking fountain on the left, erected in 1888, with the words - " *Drink Pilgrims here.*" Turn right and before the cafe, left - Finsbury Park 3 miles. Follow the path which later bears right past a Conservation Area, and down to New Gate entrance - another "nature gate". Cross Muswell Hill road (B550) and enter Queens Wood. Pass almost immediately on your left the cafe and bear right and descend. Soon follow the path uphill, then leftwards along a level section before bearing right along the path to Queens Wood Road. Go straight across and reach the Capital Ring path sign - Finsbury Park 2 1/2 miles. Keep straight ahead along the path through the wood and later follow it right down and then up steps to reach the road - Priory Gardens.

Turn right and at house no. 65 turn left - 115 yards ahead is Highgate Underground Station. Ascend to Shepherds Hill (road), beside Highgate Library. Turn right to the main road - Archway (A1) and turn left; there are shops and cafe here. In a few yards turn left to reach the former railway line, between Finsbury Park and Alexandra Palace. Turn right along it - Parkland Walk - Finsbury Park is now 2 1/4 miles away - you are halfway! In less than a mile pass under the road bridge at Crouch End (A103). Finsbury Park is 1 1/2 miles and Highgate Wood is 1 1/2 miles. Pass the former station platform and soon keep right past a play area, along the rail bed. 1/4 mile late pass under the A1201 - Crouch Hill. Continue straight ahead along the former railway line, with bluebells and gorse growing in early summer. Later pass near Stroud Green as the path curves right to its end.

Turn left and cross the railway line and into Finsbury Park, with Finsbury Park Station 1/4 mile to your right. Keep straight ahead to pass the park Cafe and boating lake and play area. Follow the tarmaced path to the Makenzie Pavilion. Keep left to walk through the Makenzie Gardens - made in 1870. At the end reach a shelter and turn right for Manor House Station - 250 yards away.

Follow the tarmaced path to the main road - Green Lanes and station.

If continuing along the New River section (next walk); at the shelter keep left along the path before turning right and descending to a park entrance and New River. Before it turn left on the drive - see next section.

HIGHGATE WOOD - Originally named Gravel Pit Wood, was once part of the Forest of Middlesex. Bought in the 19th. century and opened to the public in 1886, by the Corporation of London. Like other areas, including Epping Forest, the land was aquired by the Corporation for use in perpetuity of Londoners.

Highgate Wood.

QUEENS WOOD - Formerley known as Churchyard Bottom Wood, and later renamed after Queen Victoria. One of four ancient woodlands in the Borough of Haringey. The other three are - Highgate Wood, Coldfall Wood and Bluebell Wood.

PARKLAND WALK - Is one of three Local Nature Reserves in the Borough of Haringey. The other two are Queens Wood and Railway Fields.

FORMER RAILWAY LINE - A four mile spur line from Finsbury Park via Highgate to Alexandra Palace was made in 1867. The final section to Alexandra Palace was completed in 1873. The last passenger train ran in 1954, but the line remained opened to freight traffic until 1971. In 1984 the Parkland Walk was opened. You can walk to Alexandra Palace from Queens Wood along the Capital Ring and then rejoining the Parkland Walk to Muswell Hill and into The Grove and Alexandra Park - see separate walk.

Capital Ring sign in Highgate Wood, near Cafe.

THE CAPITAL RING - as the walk's logo explains, it is a 78 mile circular - Recreational Path - around central London - both north and south of the Thames and basically within ten miles of Big Ben. It is well worth walking it all and seeing many fascinating places in the capital city. As you walk this route you will see the walks' logo and signs, helping to confirm that your are walking the right way!

I walked the ring over five days; it would have been 4 days but for a 30°C heat wave!

My walk schedule is as follows -

North Woolwich to Crystal Palace - 17 miles

Crystal Palace to Richmond - 17 miles

Richmond to Preston Road - 17 miles

Preston Road to Manor House - 13 miles

Manor House to North Woolwich - 14 miles

Capital Ring sign on the Parkland Walk.

17

THE NEW RIVER IN HARINGEY
- 4 1/2 MILES

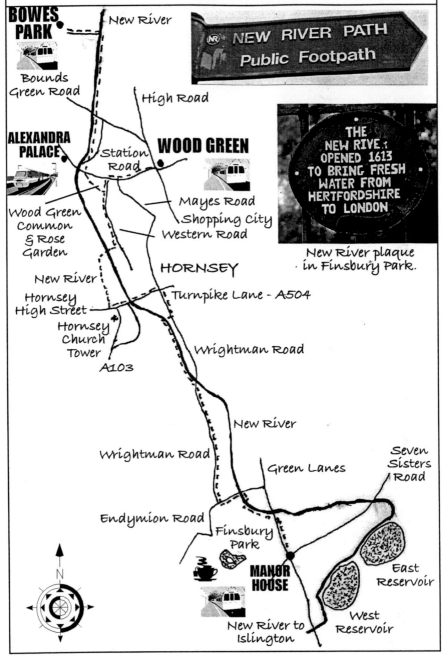

BOWES PARK

New River

NEW RIVER PATH
Public Footpath

Bounds Green Road

High Road

ALEXANDRA PALACE

Station Road

WOOD GREEN

THE NEW RIVER OPENED 1613 TO BRING FRESH WATER FROM HERTFORDSHIRE TO LONDON

Wood Green Common & Rose Garden

Mayes Road

Shopping City

Western Road

New River plaque in Finsbury Park.

HORNSEY

New River

Hornsey High Street

Turnpike Lane - A504

Hornsey Church Tower

A103

Wrightman Road

New River

Wrightman Road

Green Lanes

Seven Sisters Road

Endymion Road

Finsbury Park

MANOR HOUSE

East Reservoir

West Reservoir

N

New River to Islington

18

THE NEW RIVER IN HARINGEY
- 4 1/2 MILES - allow 2 hours.

Basic route - Manor House Station - Finsbury Park - New River - Wrightman Road - New River - Wrightman Road - Hornsey - Hornsey Church Tower - New River - Western Road - Wood Green Common - Station Road - Wood Green.

Extension to Bowes Park - 1 mile - Wood Green Common - New River - Myddleton Road - Bowes Park Station.

Map - O.S. 1:25,000 Explorer Series No. 173 - London North.

Start - Manor House Underground Station - Piccadilly Line. Bus Nos. 29, 253, 254, 259.

End - Wood Green Underground Station - Piccadilly Line. Bus nos. 29, 67, 121, 123, 141, 144, 184, 221, 230, 232, 329, W4.

Alternative endings at Alexandra Palace Rail Station and Bounds Green Underground Station (Piccadilly Line).

INNS - The Great Northern Railway Tavern, Hornsey High Road - just off the route. Several around Wood Green.

Cafe - several around Wood Green.

ABOUT THE WALK - This end to end walk follows the New River in the borough from the south to north. The walk can also be added to the Capital Ring walk - see previous walk. It also forms part of a 12 mile circular walk - see next walk for details.

The New River is/was a major early 17th. century undertaking to bring fresh water, 40 miles from Chadwell Springs near Hertford to Islington. The walk follows the "river", where practicable and is a delightful haven running through the northern heart of the Capital. The river is home to coots, moorhens, mallards, mute swans and Canada geese. Just off the route in Hornsey is the Hornsey church tower which is well worth a visit; a piece of 15th. century is surrounding suburbia. The route also coincides with the Piccadilly Line, above ground.

WALKING INSTRUCTIONS - Starting from Manor House Station, cross the main road - Green Lanes, A105 - into Finsbury Park. Immediately turn right and keep to the righthand side of the park along the drive. As it curves left, a wide path on the left descends to join cross the drive - this is the path from the previous walk for those joining the Capital Ring and New River together. Follow the drive, now with the New River on your right to where you can turn right and cross it. Here on the right can be seen the oldest plaque on the river, shown on the map. Cross the river and follow the path left to Endymion Road. For the next 3/4 mile you cannot walk beside the river, as it passes through dense housing.

Turn left and soon right along Alroy Road, after crossing the railway line this road becomes Wrightman Road. Follow it for 1/2 mile, passing Stroud Green Station on the left and St. Paul's church on the right. At house no. 20, turn left and rejoin the New River; cross a footbridge and walk beside it on your right. In 1/4 mile reach a road and turn right to pass a mosque on your left and regain Wrightman Road. Turn left past various religious buildings of different faiths to a road junction - Turnpike Lane - A504. Turn left and pass the West Indian Cultural Centre and pass under the railway bridge. Soon after the New River is on your right; because of building work access is a little further along the road - along the drive on the right into the St. James development. Before turning, just ahead is the Great Northern Railway Tavern and shops of Hornsey High Road, and on the left Hornsey Church Tower.

Keep straight ahead through the St. James development. Pass The Pump house, dated 1903 and keep ahead along Shadwell Avenue. At the end of the road reach a fenced path and turn right and cross the New River and follow the path left beside it before bearing right to walk through a railway tunnel to Western Road. Turn left and pass the Alexandra Primary School on the right, and later on the left The Decorium. Just after the path forks. The New River path turns left to walk beside Wood Green Common. While the road keeps ahead on the right of it to Station Road. If walking to Wood Green follow this to Station Road and turn right. Keep along it to Wood Green Station and Wood Green High Road; Shopping City is to your right.

If continuing along the New River Path, keep left along the path to Station Road, with the football field (Wood Green Common) on the right. At Station Road to your left is Alexandra Station and the final part of the circular walk through Alexandra park back to East Finchley - see next walk for details. To continue along the New River cross the road into Avenue Gardens with the river on your right. It soon disappears underground, but simply keep straight ahead through the gardens to Bounds Green Road. Go straight across and continue in gardens to Finsbury Road. Turn left along this to a road junction with Truro Road. Cross and continue along Palmerston Road and take the first road on your left - Myddleton Road - named after the builder of the river and reach Bowes Green Station.

HORNSEY CHURCH TOWER AND GRAVEYARD

- The tower is the only piece of the medieval church, dedicated to St. Mary of Hornsey, left standing. The lower part was built in 1500 and in 1832 it was heightened when the church was rebuilt. The style is Gothic Revival and designed by the architect, George Smith. In 1888/9 a much larger church built beside it, with the old tower being used as the bell tower for the new church. For forty years they stood together until 1926 when the church, but not the tower was demolished. In 1969 the Victorian church was demolished leaving the tower we see today. The site of Victorian church is now occupied by St. Mary's Infant School, opposite.

On the west wall of the tower can be seen two weathered figures of angels with shields, to two previous bishops. Both of whom, were Bishops of London and owners of the Manor of Hornsey. Bishop Savage (1500) on the left and on the right Bishop Warham. There are two poets buried in the churchyard. The prominent one is near the road and surrounded by metal railings to Samuel Rogers who died in 1885. The other is to a Dutch poet who died in 1858. Another grave is of particular interest being to Harret Long and his servant, who was a slave in America; both died in 1841. The current parish church is about 3/4 miles further along the road, westwards.

New River in Finsbury Park.

NEW RIVER - some brief history notes.

As many historical notice boards along the river state - It is not a river, nor is it new. It is a remarkable piece of 17th. century engineering to bring clean water to London, some 400 years ago. Originally 40 miles long from Chadwell Spring near Hertford, to the New River Head in Islington, London; close to Saddler's Wells Theatre. The "river" hugs the 100 foot contour line, often doing loops to maintain height, such as around Forty Hall and Enfield Town. Today it is 24 miles long, with the loops omitted by taking the water through pipes and tunnels. The aim behind the 100 foot contour line, was so water could then be gravity fed to the houses of the City of London. The water fell 11 1/2 inches per mile.

A water channel was proposed in 1600 and an Act of 1606 basically set up the

22

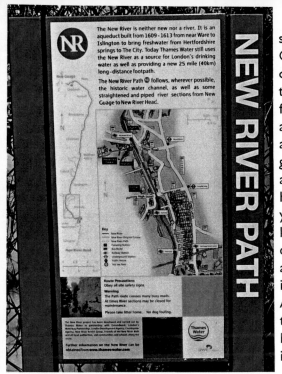

The New River is neither new nor a river. It is an aqueduct built from 1609 - 1613 from near Ware to Islington to bring freshwater from Hertfordshire springs to The City. Today Thames Water still uses the New River as a source for London's drinking water as well as providing a new 25 mile (40km) long-distance footpath.

The New River Path **NR** follows, wherever possible, the historic water channel, as well as some straightened and piped river sections from New Guage to New River Head.

NEW RIVER PATH

scheme. Originally Edmund Colhurst, who had proposed the channel, was to undertake the task. However concerns over financing, the council accepted an offer from Hugh Myddleton, a welshman, who was a London goldsmith and a former M.P. He agreed to finance the project himself and complete it on four years. Hugh Myddleton was knighted in October 1612 and died on December 10th. 1631 and a statue to him can be seen in Islington close to Camden Antique Market, unveiled by the then Chancellor of the Exchequer, William Gladstone in 1862.

Work began at Chadwell Spring on April 21st. 1609 and was completed more than four years later on September 29th. 1613 - the Lord Mayor of London officially opened the waterway on this day. The cost of construction is believed to be £18,527. 0d. 1d. The "river" was basically 10 feet wide and 4 feet deep. Puddled clay was used as a liner to make it waterproof. Over its 40 mile length the water falls 18 ft. - 5 1/2 inches a mile. 157 bridges were built along its path for roads and paths across the "river".

In the first year 175 houses were using the water supply and the following year this had doubled. By 1809 it was 59,058 houses and by 1834 this had risen to 73,212. As the demand for water increased reservoirs were built at Cheshunt and the East and West Reservoirs at Stoke Newington.

The New River is still used by Thames Water Board; the river being fed mostly by the River Lee, which rises near Luton. Originally the New River was fed by the springs at Chadwell and Amwell, who combined provided a maximum of 10 megalitres a day. A statue in 1738 allowed upto 102 megalitres to be taken from the River Lee. More than century later these amounts were doubled. Today, more than 38 million gallons of water, a day, is brought to London along this "river."

For a full in depth look at the New River, see Michael Essex-Lopresti book - *"Exploring The New River."*

EAST FINCHLEY CIRCULAR WALK
- 12 MILES - ALEXANDRA PARK
TO EAST FINCHLEY.

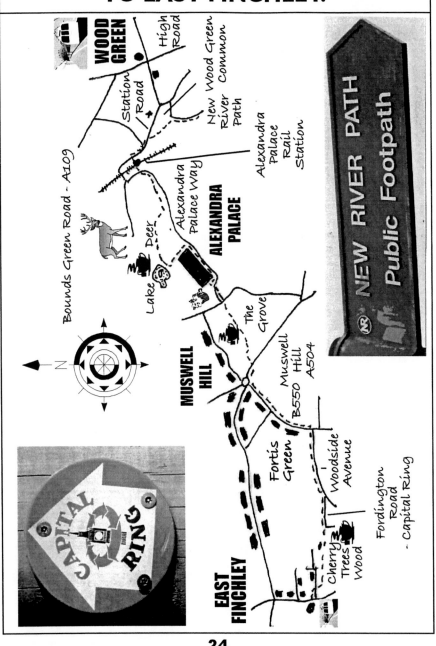

EAST FINCHLEY 12 MILE CIRCULAR WALK
- using the Capital Ring, New River and Alexandra Park.
- allow 5 hours.

Basic route - East Finchley - Capital Ring - Cherry Tree Woods - Highgate Wood - Queens Wood - Parkland Walk - Finsbury Park - New River - Hornsey - Alexandra Palace Station - Alexandra Park - The Grove - Muswell Hill - Fortis Green - Capital Ring - Cherry Tree Wood - East Finchley.

Map - O.S. 1:25,000 Explorer Series No. 173 - London North.

<u>Start and end</u> at East Finchley Underground Station - Northern Line, High Barnet branch.
Bus nos. 143, 234, & 263.

Inns - The Great Northern Railway Tavern, Hornsey High Road, just off the route. The Phoenix Inn, Alexandra Palace. Several inns in Muswell Hill.

Cafe - Park Cafe in Cherry Tree Woods - The Lazy Sally; Highgate Woods, just off the route and in Finsbury Park. Lake cafe in Alexandra Park. Cafe in The Grove. Several cafe's in Muswell Hill.

ABOUT THE WALK - This is a delightful walk of great variety and a combination using two other walks in this book - The Capital Ring (Pages 12 to 17) and New River in Haringey, (Pages 18 to 23). Near Wood Green, you keep left for Alexandra Palace Station and begin the final leg of the walk through Alexandra Palace. Here you have views over London's skyline before walking through The Grove to Muswell Hill. A short road walk brings you back to your start along the Capital Ring at Cherry Tree Woods. You can walk it in stages, as you pass several underground stations and numerous bus routes.

WALKING INSTRUCTIONS - Use the walking instructions already detailed, with maps, - The Capital Ring in Haringey - 4 1/2 miles and The New River in Haringey - 4 1/2 miles. As detailed in the latter walk, reaching Wood Green Common, keep left along the New River signed path to Station Road. Here leave the New River and turn left along the road to Alexandra Palace Station. Immediately after the station's entrance turn left across the footbridge to Bedford Road. Turn left and in a few yards, right to follow the tarmaced path above the Alexandra Palace Way. Reaching a drive close to the road, turn right and follow it round to your left to pass the Deer enclosure and then boating lake with a cafe on your right. Turn left and walk past the car park and northern end of Alexandra Palace. Reaching the promenade, turn right and walk past the building on the right with views of the London skyline on the left.

At the end of the building bear right and opposite the Palm Court Entrance and Phoenix Bar, turn left down steps to the road. Keep right along it for a few yards before turning right onto a tarmaced path to walk through The Grove. As you do so pass the cafe. At the end bear left and walk along the bridge to Muswell Hill. Turn right and ascend briefly to the main roundabout. Turn left along Muswell Hill Broadway. Ignore the first right turning - Fortis Green Road. Keep straight ahead along the B550 - Muswell Hill Road in Fortis Green, and take the next road on the right - Woodside Avenue. Little over 1/4 mile along here you return to familiar territory. Turn right along Fordington Avenue and rejoin the Capital Ring. Where the road turns left, keep straight ahead into Cherry Tree Wood. Pass the Lazy Sally Cafe and at the end of the park exit on the right to Brompton Road. Turn left and in a few strides you are back opposite East Finchley Station.

Alexandra Palace from the New River in Hornsey.

Fallow Deer in Alexandra Park Enclosure.

ALEXANDRA PALACE & PARK - 3 MILES

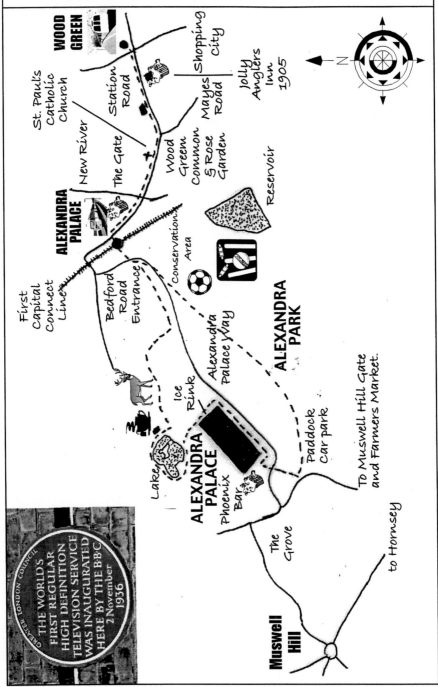

ALEXANDRA PALACE AND PARK - 3 MILES - allow 2 hours.

Basic route - *Wood Green Underground Station - Station Road - Alexandra Palace Station - Bedford Road Entrance - Alexandra Park - Deer Enclosure - Boating Lake - Alexandra Palace - Bedford Road Entrance - Alexandra Palace Station - Wood Green.*

Map - O.S. 1:25,000 Explorer Series No. 173 - London North.

<u>*Start and end*</u> - *Wood Green Underground Station - Piccadilly Line.*
<u>*Alternative*</u> - *Alexandra Palace Station - Moorgate/First Capital Connect.*
Buses - No. 144 - Wood Green Station. No. W3 - Alexandra Palace Station and Palace/Park.

Inns - Goose Inn & Jolly Anglers Inn, Wood Green. The Gate Inn opposite Alexandra Palace Station. Phoenix Bar, Alexandra Palace.

Cafe - Lakeside cafe, Alexandra Park. Public Toilets are adjacent the cafe. Boat hire during the season.

ABOUT THE WALK - Alexandra Palace is one of major landmarks of north London and provides a stunning vantage over the city's skyline. It is also the place where the BBC Television Service began. The walk can be done as part of a shopping trip to Shopping City in Wood Green or as a Sunday visit to the Farmers Market (10.a.m - 3.0 p.m.) at the Muswell Hill entrance to the park. The walk is an enjoyable walk in its own right, with a steady gentle climb to the Palace. En route passing the fallow deer enclosure and walking around the lake. After you walk beside the palace with uninterrupted views over the city. You descend and walk along the parks eastern side back to the Bedford Road entrance and retrace your steps back to your start. I have described the longer walk from Wood Green Station, which passes Alexandra Palace Station; if starting from there it is about a 2 mile circuit.

WALKING INSTRUCTIONS - Starting from Wood Green Station, cross the road to Station Road opposite, with The Goose Inn on the left. Walk along Station Road and pass the Jolly Anglers Inn (1905) on the left and later on the right Greenside House. Soon after follow the road right - still on Station Road - with Mayes Road on your left. Also on your left is the Wood Green Common and Rose Garden. Pass St. Paul's Catholic Church on the right, which has, *"Our Lady Fatima (Portugal)"*, in a window. Soon after cross the New River and park on the right. A little further as you ascend gently reach Alexandra Palace Station and The gate Inn opposite.

Turn left across the footbridge past the platforms and over the railway line to the road - Bedford Road - beyond. Turn left and in a few yards keep to the righthand side of the road to follow a tarmaced path away from the road, but parallel to it, as you enter Alexandra Park. On your left is the tarmaced drive - Alexandra Palace Way - you will return to it later. First follow the ascending path to a drive and turn right. It soon curves left as you pass the fallow deer enclosure on the right. Continue on the drive ascending to the Lake and turn right to walk around it. Now near the summit of the "hill" and pass the cafe and boat hire. Follow the path around the lake to near to where first reached the path. Turn right to walk past the car parking area and ice rink area of Alexandra Palace. Gaining the promenade turn right, passing the BBC plaque on the right and others, as you walk beside the palace to its other end. On your left you have stunning views to London's skyline and Canary Wharf - see cover photograph.

At the end of the building curve right past the Phoenix Bar and opposite the Palm Court entrance, turn left down steps. to the road - Alexandra Palace Way. if you turn right here and follow it left you will come to the Muswell Hill Entrance, here a Farmers Market is held here on Sundays - 10 a.m. to 3.0 p.m. Continuing on the walk, cross the road to a path and descend. At the bottom turn left, along the road & path, signed - Wood Green 1 1/4 miles. The road and path lead towards the Paddock Car Park. Near the entrance keep left - path signed Wood Green 1 1/4 miles - you haven't walked far from the last one! The tarmaced path becomes a drive and follow it all the way back to the Bedford Road Entrance. As you do so on your right is a cricket field, a football fields and near the entrance a Conservation area, which a side path allows you to explore.

Back at the road you came in on, turn right and a few yards later right over the footbridge to Alexandra Palace Station. Turn right along Station Road and retrace your steps back to Wood Green. Pass the New River and St. Paul's

30

church and keep left, still on Station Road, to pass the Jolly Anglers Inn and regain High Road and Wood Green Station.

The Jolly Anglers Inn, 1905, Station Road, Wood Green.

ALEXANDRA PALACE - Known as *"the People's Palace"*, it is north London's equivalent to the Crystal Palace. The success of the latter resulted in many other "Palace's" being built throughout the world. Two experts who worked on the Crystal Palace also worked here.; the designer, Owen Jones and the engineer Sir Charles Fox. The park covering 196 acres was made in 1863 and building was built between 1865/6 and cost £417,128. The Park was opened to the public in 1866 and the Palace was officially opened on Queen Victoria's birthday. May 25th. 1873. The rail line - "The Muswell Hill and Palace Railway" - was opened on 2nd. June 1873, and 60,00 visited the Palace that day. A 17 brick arched aqueduct crosses St. James Lane.

Within the first sixteen days 124,000 people visited the Palace. Inside the Great Hall could seat 12,000 people and the organ by Henry Willis was the largest in the country. A serious fire in the dome on the seventeenth day, badly gutted the building. Rebuilding work commenced immediately and the Palace was opened again in 1875, as an exhibition and concert centre. In 1934 the south-eastern part was leased to the B.B.C. and two years later the world's first regular television service was broadcast from here, on November 2nd. 1936; the year the TV mast was added.

In 1980, the trusteeship of the park and palace was transferred to the Haringey Council and six months later fate struck again as a fire on 10th. July 1980 badly damaged the building. The Great Hall was rebuilt and today it is still a popular Exhibition Centre, with an ice rink, Palm Court room and bar. Plaques on the building record its history. Between 1914 - 1919, 17,000 German prisoners of war were interned here. Another is to Henry Burt J. P., who first proposed the Park and Palace be bought for the people. Through his effort the Park was opened to the public on the 18th. May 1901.

Alexander Mackenzie included a deer enclosure in his plan in 1875. Fallow Deer were introduced and their descendants live here today. The view from the Palace over London is one of north London's finest vantage points.

1914-1919

THIS PLAQUE WAS PLACED HERE ON SUNDAY 4 JUNE 2000 BY MEMBERS OF THE ANGLO-GERMAN FAMILY HISTORY SOCIETY TO REMEMBER OVER 17,000 GERMAN AND OTHER CIVILIAN PRISONERS OF WAR INTERNED AT ALEXANDRA PALACE BETWEEN 1914 AND 1919, IN PARTICULAR THOSE WHO DIED DURING THAT PERIOD

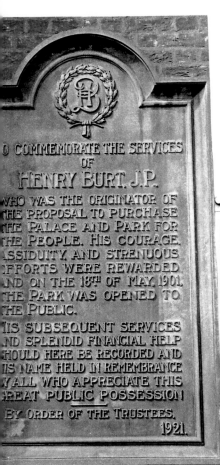

TO COMMEMORATE THE SERVICES OF

HENRY BURT. J.P.

WHO WAS THE ORIGINATOR OF THE PROPOSAL TO PURCHASE THE PALACE AND PARK FOR THE PEOPLE. HIS COURAGE, ASSIDUITY AND STRENUOUS EFFORTS WERE REWARDED AND ON THE 18TH OF MAY 1901 THE PARK WAS OPENED TO THE PUBLIC.

HIS SUBSEQUENT SERVICES AND SPLENDID FINANCIAL HELP SHOULD HERE BE RECORDED AND HIS NAME HELD IN REMEMBRANCE BY ALL WHO APPRECIATE THIS GREAT PUBLIC POSSESSION

BY ORDER OF THE TRUSTEES.

1921.

GREATER LONDON COUNCIL

THE WORLD'S FIRST REGULAR HIGH DEFINITION TELEVISION SERVICE WAS INAUGURATED HERE BY THE B·B·C 2 November 1936

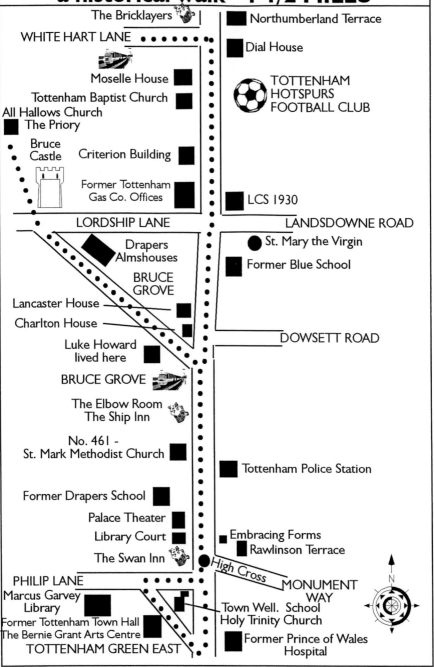

TOTTENHAM, HIGH ROAD
a historical walk - 1 1/2 MILES

The Bricklayers

Northumberland Terrace

WHITE HART LANE

Dial House

Moselle House

TOTTENHAM
HOTSPURS
FOOTBALL CLUB

Tottenham Baptist Church

All Hallows Church
The Priory

Bruce
Castle   Criterion Building

Former Tottenham
Gas Co. Offices   LCS 1930

LORDSHIP LANE   LANDSDOWNE ROAD

St. Mary the Virgin

Drapers
Almshouses   Former Blue School

BRUCE
GROVE

Lancaster House

Charlton House

DOWSETT ROAD

Luke Howard
lived here

BRUCE GROVE

The Elbow Room
The Ship Inn

No. 461 -
St. Mark Methodist Church

Tottenham Police Station

Former Drapers School

Palace Theater

Library Court   Embracing Forms
Rawlinson Terrace

The Swan Inn

High Cross

PHILIP LANE   MONUMENT
WAY

Marcus Garvey
Library   Town Well. School

Former Tottenham Town Hall   Holy Trinity Church
The Bernie Grant Arts Centre

TOTTENHAM GREEN EAST   Former Prince of Wales
Hospital

N

Start - *White Hart Lane Train Station.*
Bus no. W3.

End - *High Cross area, Tottenham Green. Bus nos. 123, 259, 279, 349, 476, W4.*

Inns - The Bricklayers Inn, The Elbow Room, The Ship Inn and The Swan Inn, Tottenham High Road.

ABOUT THE WALK - This is simply a walk along Tottenham High Road to look at some of the interesting buildings that survive along this road. There is an option to explore Bruce Grove and Castle, the former village area of Tottenham. Tottenham's name is said to be named after the ancient Druid God - Teutates. There was possibly a shrine where the High Cross stands today. The High Road follows the line of the Roman Road, Ermine Street, which is why it is straight. The road, was one of the Roman's most important in Britain, running from London, via Lincoln and York to Hadrian's Wall. For the last 300 years it has been a popular thoroughfare lined with buildings - houses, shops and businesses.

Haringey Borough was created from three Middlesex borough's of Hornsey, Tottenham and Wood Green. In 1995 the population of the borough was 213,500. The population of Tottenham in 1861 as 13,240. In 1891 - 97, 174 and in 1931 - 157,752.

WALKING INSTRUCTIONS AND HISTORY NOTES - From White Hart Lane Station, turn right to Tottenham High Road. To your left is The Bricklayers Inn and Northumberland Terrace. Almost opposite is the Dial House. Turn right to walk along High Road.

DIAL HOUSE - There are several 18th. century buildings in this area; three storeys high with a basement. No. 790 - Dial House with a sun dial high up, dated 1691. Nos. 794-784, Northumberland Terrace were built between 1750/2.

Dial House and sundial detail.

Continue along the righthand side of the road passing The Moselle House, set back from the road and Tottenham Baptist Church. The lefthand side is dominated by the Premiership, Tottenham Hotspurs Football Club. Further pass on the right above the shops, the Criterion Building and as you approach Lordship Lane, on your right is the red bricked building, now occupied by the North Tottenham Community Services.

No. 639 - NORTH TOTTENHAM COMMUNITY SERVICES - Formerly the Tottenham Gas Company offices built in 1907 - 1914; the date stones are high up. Designed in Edwardian Jacobean style with intricate embellishments.

Opposite on the corner of Landsdowne Road is -

LCS 1930 - White classical corner turret of the former Co-operative Wholesale Society department store; now Allied Carpets. A short distance down Landsdowne Road on the right is St. Mary the Virgin church, built 1885-7.

A little further down the High Road on the left is -

No. 614-620 - Beside Scotland Green is the curved brick gables of the former Blue School; a girl's charity school built in 1833 by Samuel Angell, and enlarged in 1876. In 1886 the school was known as The Tottenham Middle School which closed in 1930.

A little further on the righthand side is -

No. 583-585 - LANCASTER HOUSE - A pair of 18th. century three storey houses with four bays each, with large red bricked pilasters. Next door is -

CHARLTON HOUSE - A smaller 18th. century "cottage" with a Doric door case.

Just after is Bruce Grove and station - side trip can be made up here; see separate section below.

Continue along High Road passing The Elbow Inn and Ship Inn.

THE SHIP INN - Tottenham High Road - The earlier building was frequently visited by the famous fisherman, Izaak Walton, who often fished on the River Lee. He is renowned for his book, The Complete Angler. An inn is known to have existed here in 1455.

A little further on the right above the shops is -

No. 461 - ST. MARK METHODIST CHURCH - The church was originally built in 1867 and considerably remodelled in 1963. The prominent grey Art Dec Tower was built in 1937.

On the other side of the road is the police station -

TOTTENHAM POLICE STATION - Neo Georgian style built in 1913.

Back on the right is Drapers Road and at the top is -

OLD SCHOOL COURT - Drapers Road - Gothic style built between 1860-2. Originally Drapers College for Boys in 1858. Between 1885 - 1985 was the Tottenham High School for Girls. Renovated in private dwellings in 1998.

Back on the High Road on the right is -

TOTTENHAM PALACE THEATRE - built in 1908 and has an impressive Neo-Baroque front - see datestone. Inside is seating for 1,500 people. In 1926 became a cinema and a Bingo Hall in 1969; closed in 19809's.

Just after is Library Court whose front dates from 1896. On the other side of the road is -

THE EMBRACING FORMS - A stone sculpture by Vanessa Pomeroy and purchased in 1983. Behind is the white painted and turreted, Rawlinson Terrace.

Rawlinson Terrace.

40

Straight ahead is The Swan Inn and -

HIGH CROSS - A wooden wayside cross is recorded to be here in 1409. In the 17th. century a brick structure was built. In the 19th. century this restored and given a Gothic outer, being polygonal is shape with a conical top.

HIGH CROSS PUMP - Sunk in 1791 by Thomas Smith, Lord of the Manor. For a long while it was Tottenham's only source of drinking water. The well head, gears and conical roof date from 1876.

TOTTENHAM HIGH CROSS

THIS MONUMENT STANDS ON THE SITE OF A MEDIEVAL WAYSIDE CROSS WHICH WAS REBUILT IN BRICK IN ABOUT 1600 BY DEAN WOOD, A LOCAL RESIDENT AND DEAN OF ARMAGH. IN 1809 THE VILLAGERS OF TOTTENHAM RAISED MONEY FOR ITS RENOVATION IN ITS PRESENT FORM AND THE STRUCTURE IS NOW MAINTAINED BY HARINGEY COUNCIL.

Behind is a Gothic School building and Holy Trinity church; both built in the 19th. century.

Turn right along Philip Lane, along its lefthand side and before the Tottenham Green Leisure centre and Marcus Garvey Library founded on August 7th. 1987. Marking the centenary anniversary of Brother Marcus Mosiah Garvey, an Afrikan born in Jamaica, West Indies on August 17th. 1887. He brought about the, *"Regenerating black pride, self reliance and confidence."*

Turn left to pass the former Tottenham County School, dated 1913 at the top and with a Commemorative stone dated 1912 at the bottom. Next door is the Bernie Grants Art Gallery and Tottenham Town Hall.

TOTTENHAM TOWN HALL - made from brick and stone and built in 1905 is Baroque style, designed by A. S. Taylor and R. Jemmett. They also did the former fire station on the left and the Public Baths on the right, of which only the front remains - now the Bernie Grant Arts Centre.

Continue along Tottenham Town Hall Approach, with wooded green on the left back to High Road beside the War Memorial on the left. Cross the road and small park to reach your last building with a large white Fleur de Lys on the porch.

FORMER HOSPITAL - Founded in 1868 as the Deaconesses' Institute. Large four storey Neo Georgian building, built in 1881. In 1899 became Tottenham Hospital and in 1907, the Prince of Wales Hospital; hence the fleur de lys. Converted to flats in 1992.

Turn left along the road back to the High Road and cross over towards the High Cross and bus stops.

BRUCE GROVE ONE WAY WALK EXTENSION -

Walk up Bruce Grove and pass several 19th. century Georgian "Gentleman's" residences on the left. One No. 7 has a blue plaque to Luke Howard, the namer of clouds, lived and died here - 1772 - 1864. Opposite is the former Bruce Grove Cinema. A picture taken in 1893 of this road shows the tree lined street and fine houses on the left and open fields on the right.

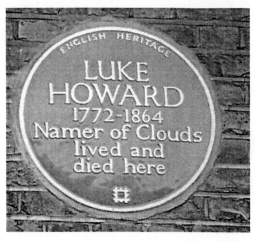

LUKE HOWARD - A Quaker chemist. meteorologist, philanthropist and founder of Howard & Sons. In the early 19th. century he lived at Chesterton House, Balam Street, Plaistow before moving here.

In 1803 he published his work on cloud classification, which he had devised. He named and distinguished three principal types of clouds -

> **Cirrus** - High Clouds.
> **Cumulus** - a heap or a pile of clouds.
> **Stratus** - Spread out of flatten out.

His observations and classification have formed the basis of modern work on clouds. Today there are now ten basic genera.

Towards the top on the right are the -

DRAPERS ALMSHOUSES - A combination of three city foundations here to the countryside and the three sided complex with central chapel was designed and built by Herbert Williams in 1868/9.

At the top, cross the road - Lordship Lane - into Bruce Castle Park.

BRUCE CASTLE - named after medieval times when the area was owned by Robert Bruce. In 1514 the estate was acquired by Sir William Compton and an E shaped mansion was built. Lord Coleraine was a later owner and he updated and enlarged the building. In the south west corner is a circular brick tower, 21 feet in diameter. It is not known what it's purpose was and was built in the early 16th. century. In 1892 the park was opened to the public, becoming Tottenham's first public park. In the grounds can be seen ancient oak tree. From 1906 the building became a museum and archives department, first for Tottenham and then for the Borough of Haringey.

The circular tower has a sad tale about it. Lord Coleraine is said to have locked up his second wife in the tower. She escaped by jumping off the top with a baby. Her ghost is said to haunt the tower and each year in November she repeats her jump!

Walk past the museum following the path passing it on the left to reach Church Lane. Turn right and pass on the left -

THE PRIORY - Church Lane, has been the Vicarage from 1906. The east front is Georgian with five bays. in the centre is a Doric door case with segmental pediment and eaves cornice. The interior has considerable 17th. century workmanship, dating from the time when the building was owned by Joseph Fenton, a city barber-surgeon, in 1620 (Jacobean). The wrought iron gates are from the 18th. century.

The Priory Gates.

ALL HALLOWS CHURCH - Medieval church with the tower built in four stages; the earliest is dated 14th. century. Inside are 16th. century brasses and monuments from the 17th. century onwards. The graveyard contains many 18th. century tombstones. Between 1607-1632 William Bedwell the translator of the King James Bible, was vicar here.

TOTTENHAM CEMETERY - Beyond All Hallows church was opened in 1858.

By continuing along Church Lane round to your right reach Beaufoy Road. Here are the Sir William Staines Almshouses, founded in St. Giles, Cripplegate and rebuilt here in 1868.

Retrace your steps back to Bruce Grove and down it to Tottenham High Road.

Tottenham Hotspurs - Spurs - Football Ground, White Hart Lane.
Where the walk began.

SIX PARKS OF TOTTENHAM - 7 MILES

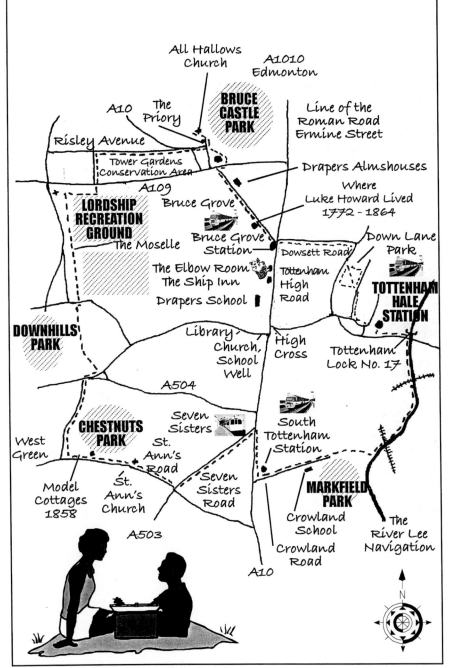

All Hallows Church

A1010 Edmonton

The Priory

A10

BRUCE CASTLE PARK

Line of the Roman Road Ermine Street

Risley Avenue

Tower Gardens Conservation Area

Drapers Almshouses

A109

Where Luke Howard Lived 1772 - 1864

Bruce Grove

LORDSHIP RECREATION GROUND

The Moselle

Bruce Grove Station

Dowsett Road

Down Lane Park

The Elbow Room The Ship Inn

Tottenham High Road

TOTTENHAM HALE STATION

Drapers School

DOWNHILLS PARK

Library Church, School Well

High Cross

Tottenham Lock No. 17

A504

Seven Sisters

South Tottenham Station

CHESTNUTS PARK

West Green

St. Ann's Road

Seven Sisters Road

MARKFIELD PARK

Model Cottages 1858

St. Ann's Church

A503

Crowland School

Crowland Road

A10

The River Lee Navigation

N

SIX PARKS OF TOTTENHAM
- 7 MILES
- allow 3 hours

Basic route - Tottenham Hale Station - Tottenham Lock - River Lee Navigation - Markfield Park - South Tottenham Station - Seven Sisters Road - St. Ann's Road and Church - Chestnuts Park - Downhills Park - Lordship Recreation Ground - Tower Gardens Conservation Area - Bruce Castle Park - Bruce Grove - Tottenham High Road - Dowsett Road - Down Lane Park - Tottenham Hale Station.

Map - O.S. 1:25,000 Explorer Series No. 173 - London North.

Start/End - Tottenham Hale Station - rail line and Underground - Piccadilly Line & Victoria Line.
Bus nos. 41, 123, 230, W4.

The route also passes South Tottenham Station, Seven Sisters (Victoria Line) and Bruce Grove Station.

Inns - The Elbow Room and The Ship, just off the route in Tottenham High Road.

Cafe - Chestnuts Park. Cafe in Lordship Lane.

ABOUT THE WALK - In the Tottenham area are several excellent parks and this walk brings you to six of them. As you walk between the parks you pass several historical buildings. You begin by walking a small section of the River Lee Navigation, southwards, to your first park - Markfield Park. From there road walking brings you past St. Ann's Church and Model Cottages, dated 1858, to Chestnuts Park. Here you head northwards walking through three parks, Chestnuts, Downhills Park and the Lordship Recreation Ground. A brief walk through the Tower Gardens Conservation Area brings you to Bruce's Castle Park and Museum. Next you walk along Bruce Grove past Almshouses and historic plaques to Tottenham High Road. After crossing the road you follow Dowsett Road and Park View Road to reach your last park, Down Lane Park, a small but attractive park. A short road walk afterwards returns you to Tottenham Hale Station

WALKING INSTRUCTIONS - Starting from Tottenham Hale Station, turn left and left again to reach Ferry Lane. Cross and turn left, away from the station and Retail Park and in less than 1/3 mile (5 mins) reach the River Lee Navigation. Turn right and descend to the towpath; to your left beyond the road bridge can be seen Tottenham Lock. Follow the towpath with the navigation on your left, for little over 1/2 mile. The area is popular with rowers, as well as mute swans, Canada Geese, Coots, Moorhens and Common Terns. Pass under two railway bridges and soon after the second one, turn right into Markfield Park. Keep ahead along the wide pathway, passing on the right the Beam Engine Museum. Follow the path left and right to continue ahead passing the Children's Play Area and later the Rose Garden on the right. Just after gain Crowland Road. Keep straight ahead along it passing Crowland School to Tottenham High Road, with South Tottenham Station on the right.

View back to Tottenham Lock.

Cross the road and turn right to the next main road on the left - Seven Sisters Road - A503. Turn left and follow the road to the first rail bridge. Before it turn right along St. Ann's Road. Pass St. Ann's church - built in 1861 and restored in 1955. Just after cross Avenue Road with the Fowler Newsam Hall on the corner and beyond the Model Cottages, dated 1858. Continue along St. Ann's Road a little further and into Chestnuts Park. Keep left along the path, past the play area to near the corner and cafe. Turn right on the path and follow this northwards along the lefthand side of the park to Black Boy Road. Bear right along this road to West Green Road. Turn right and in a few yards left into Downhills Park - just ahead along the road is a grass triangle with war memorial and impressive school building dated 1899.

Follow the wide tarmaced path, at first beside a fence then a playing field on the left and later the gardens of the park on the right. As you near the road - Downhills Park Road - you have views left to Alexandra Palace. Basically go straight across the road into the Lordship Recreation Ground. Follow this tarmaced path along its lefthand side, passing gardens on the right, before crossing The Moselle stream. Keep straight ahead to the lefthand corner of the park and follow the path right to the park entrance on your left. Turn left to Lordship Lane.

Go straight across and into Walthof Avenue and now in the Tower Gardens Conservation Area. Take the second road on your right - Risley Avenue - and follow this straight ahead to the main road, The Roundway. Cross and keep right along the road to where it turns right. Here leave the road on the left to walk along All Hallows Road. Ahead is Bruce Castle Park, but first it is worth turning left to see the wrought iron gates of The Priory and All Hallows Church beyond. Return to the park entrance and enter the park, following the path right past the play area - to your left is the famous oak tree - and past Bruce Castle and Museum. If time permits it is worthwhile visiting the museum.

Reaching the road entrance beside the Holocaust Gardens, cross the road - Lordship Lane - and walk down Bruce Grove. Soon pass on the left are the Drapers Almshouses. Further down pass some interesting buildings and one on the right has a blue plaque to Luke Howard, who lived here. At the bottom reach Bruce Grove Station on the right and Tottenham High Road. To the right are two inns; one aptly named, The Elbow Room. Cross the road and turn left and in a few yards right along Dowsett Road. Follow this for little more than 1/4 mile to the fourth road on the right - Park View Road. Turn right and soon left into your last park - Down Lane Park. Keep to the path either diagonally across or you can walk either clockwise to anticlockwise to the far lefthand corner. Exit the park into Ashley Road. Keep right along this road to Hale Road. Cross and keep ahead before crossing left to regain Tottenham Hale Station.

SEVEN SISTERS - The origin of the name - According to legend, in about 1350 seven sisters planted seven elm trees around a walnut nut, before going their separate ways in life. Later a protestant martyr was burnt to death here and the walnut tree flourished but did not grow any higher. The trees are known to have been here in the 18th. century and the walnut tree died in 1790.

The Model Cottages.

ST. ANN'S ROAD - The Model Cottages and school next door were built in 1858 by Fowler Newsam, who was also the benefactor of St. Ann's church. The cottages and school have Tudor doorways and portraits in relief.

DOWNHILLS PARK - Cover 30 acres and was once part of the Mount Pleasant estate that covered 290 acres. The house was built in 1789 and demolished in 1902. In 1903 the park was created and a year later extended by four acres.

LORDSHIP RECREATION GROUND - Opened to the public in 1932.

TOWER GARDENS CONSERVATION AREA - the streets are laid out in a grid pattern and were built between 1903-1913. It becomes quite a surprise to see most houses having a privet hedge.

ALL HALLOWS CHURCH - Medieval church with the tower built in four stages; the earliest is dated 14th. century. Inside are 16th. century brasses and monuments from the 17th. century onwards. The graveyard contains many 18th. century tombstones.

TOTTENHAM CEMETERY - Beyond All Hallows church was opened in 1858.

THE PRIORY - Church Lane, has been the Vicarage from 1906. The east front is Georgian with five bays. in the centre is a Doric doorcase with segmental pediment and eaves cornice. The interior has considerable 17th. century workmanship, dating from the time when the building was owned by Joseph Fenton, a city barber-surgeon, in 1620 (Jacobean). The wrought iron gates are from the 18th. century.

Bruce Castle Park
Oak Tree.

BRUCE CASTLE - named after medieval times when the area was owned by Robert Bruce. In 1514 the estate was acquired by Sir William Compton and an E shaped mansion was built. Lord Coleraine was a later owner and he updated and enlarged the building. In the south west corner is a circular brick tower, 21 feet in diameter. It is not known what it's purpose was and was built in the early 16th. century. In 1892 the park was opened to the public, becoming Tottenham's first public park. In the grounds can be seen ancient oak tree. From 1906 the building became a museum and archives department, first for Tottenham and then for the Borough of Haringey.

DRAPERS ALMSHOUSES - A combination of three city foundations moved here, to the countryside, and the three sided complex with central chapel was designed and built by Herbert Williams in 1868/9.

LUKE HOWARD - **No. 7 Bruce Grove** - "1772 - 1864. Namer of clouds. Lived and died here."

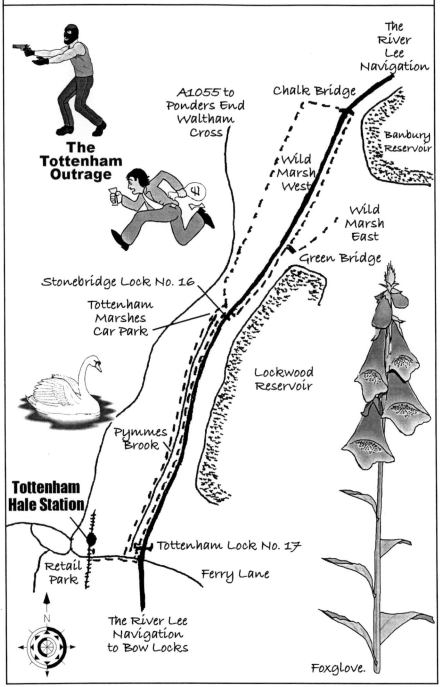

The River Lee Navigation

Chalk Bridge

A1055 to Ponders End Waltham Cross

Banbury Reservoir

The Tottenham Outrage

Wild Marsh West

Wild Marsh East

Green Bridge

Stonebridge Lock No. 16

Tottenham Marshes Car Park

Lockwood Reservoir

Pymmes Brook

Tottenham Hale Station

Tottenham Lock No. 17

Retail Park

Ferry Lane

N

The River Lee Navigation to Bow Locks

Foxglove.

TOTTENHAM MARSHES
- 4 MILES
- allow 2 hours or more.

Basic route - Tottenham Station - Ferry Lane - Pymmes Brook - Tottenham Marshes Car park - Tottenham Marshes - Wild Marsh West - Chalk Bridge - The Rive Lee Navigation - Green Bridge - Wild Marsh East - Stonebridge Lock No. 16 - Tottenham Lock No. 17 - Ferry Lane - Tottenham Hale Station.

Map - O.S. 1:25,000 Explorer Series No. 173 - London North.

<u>Start and End</u> - Tottenham Hale Station - rail line and Underground - Piccadilly Line/Victoria Line.

Bus nos. 41,123, 230, W4.

Alternative start - Tottenham Marshes Car park, off the A1055 road - Water Mead Way. Grid Ref. 352905.

Cafe - Seasonal - Stonebridge Lock.

ABOUT THE WALK - A short circular "Nature" walk around Tottenham Marshes, one of the largest Open Spaces in the area and only six miles from central London! Since 1962 about 300 different plants have been recorded in the marshes, as well sixteen different types of butterflies. There is a variety of birds to be seen with grassland types on the marsh area and waterfowl on the River Lee Navigation. Otters are known to be in the area, so keep a lookout....you never know! The Marshes and Chalk Bridge are where the two Russian wage robbers crossed in 1909, and the tragic events are known as the Tottenham Outrage.

First you walk beside the Pymmes Brook before walking around Wild Marsh West. Crossing the River Lee Navigation you head southwards beside it and have the option of exploring Wild Marsh East, as you do so. You pass Stonebridge Lock and head on to Tottenham Lock, where you leave the navigation and return to the start and station. A pair of binocular and both a flower and bird guidebook are useful aids to make this a very pleasant discovery walk.

WALKING INSTRUCTIONS - Starting from Tottenham Hale Station, turn left and left again to Ferry Lane. Keep left along the road, away from station for less than five minutes to the first path sign and kissing gate on the left - before the River Lee Navigation. Turn left onto the gravel path, signposted Stonebridge Lock 1/2 mile and Wild East Marsh 3/4 mile - both are at least 1/4 mile further than that! The path keeps near to the Pymmes Brook on your right. In 1/4 mile pass allotments on your left and continue straight ahead to Clendish Marsh. Keep straight ahead with Stonebridge Lock more than 1/4 mile away. Before it pass an informative history pillar before Tottenham Marshes Car Park. Cross the car park road, with Stonebridge Lock to your right; you will come here later.

Continue on the gravel path which swings left to the A1055 road - Water Mead Way. Bear right to cross a footbridge and follow the path away from the road before it swings left to keep along the perimeter of Wild Marsh West. Follow the path for more than 1/2 mile to the far lefthand corner of the grassland and turn right, as path signed - Chalk Bridge. Reaching the bridge over the River Lee Navigation, cross and turn right to follow the towpath with the navigation on your right. In 1/2 mile you can turn left over Green Bridge into Wild Marsh East. You can follow the path towards Banbury Reservoir, little over 1/4 mile away. Return the same way back to Green Bridge and the River Lee Navigation.

Stonebridge Lock.

Continue beside the River Lee Navigation along its towpath and in 1/4 mile reach Stonebridge Lock No. 16, and cross the bridge. To your right is the seasonal cafe, Otter Notice Board and Cycle and Canoe Centre. Turn left to continue on the towpath with the navigation now on your left. In 3/4 mile reach Tottenham Lock No. 17 and leave the navigation and reach Ferry Lane. Turn right and moments later pass your earlier path and continue on to Tottenham Hale Station on your right.

Ferry Lane Bridge and Tottenham Lock.

TOTTENHAM MARSHES - Were in the 19th. century Lammas Meadows, used for cutting hay and grazing cattle. Lammas Day was August 1st, originally celebrated as Harvest Festival.

THE TOTTENHAM OUTRAGE - On Saturday January 23rd. 1909 at about 10.30 a.m., two Russian immigrants - Jacob Lapidus and Paul Hefeld - robbed the wages bag outside Schnurmann's Rubber Works, in Chesnut Road, just off Tottenham High Road.

One of them snatched the bag containing £80.00 and a scuffle broke out. The other Russian began firing his hand gun and a local, George Smith, wrestled one of them to the ground. They got away leaving Smith lucky to be alive with bullet holes in his hat and jacket. The robbers ran off and along Dowsett Road firing frequent shots and now being chased by the police, from Tottenham Police Station, and locals.

Everyone thought the robbers would soon run out of ammunition but they kept turning round and firing at the pursers. A little boy was shot in the mouth and later died. A police car was hit several times and P.C. Tyler was shot. He later died from the head wound. In total it is estimated that the two robbers fired 400 shots; the bullets being the dum dum type - a soft nosed bullet that expands and inflicts serious wounds.

They crossed Tottenham Marshes and Chalk Bridge and took a tram at gun point. One passenger was shot in the neck. But really they had no escape and Paul Hefeld realised it was hopeless and shot himself in the head. He was taken to hospital but later died of meningitis on February 12th. 1909. Jacob Lapidus pressed on to a cottage at Oak Hill, close to Epping Forest; he was covered in blood. When the police arrived he was already dead in the front room.

During the chase hundreds of shots were fired and three people killed, including Jacob Lapidus. Fifteen people sustained bullet injuries, to arms, legs, thigh's etc. The wages bag contained £80 in gold, silver and copper. Only a small bag of £5 was found in Jacob Lapidus pocket. The remaining £75 has never been found.

RIVER LEE NAVIGATION - Some brief history notes -

Length - Limehouse Basin, Bow to Hertford - 27 3/4 miles.
19 locks.

The River Lee has been, since Roman times, an important trade route to London. An Act of 1571 for an artificial cut was made to help speed up the traffic. At the same time a pound at Waltham Abbey with lock gates - a similar principal to today - was made and is one of the earliest in the country. During the 18th and 19th. century the navigation was improved, these included in 1769 the Waltham, Edmonton and Hackney Cuts (avoiding the River Lee) and pound locks was opened. In 1911 The Lee Conservancy bought the River Stort Navigation and improved it together with the River Lee. By 1930, 130 ton boats could reach Enfield and 100 ton to Ware and Hertford. During the rest of the 20th. century many improvements were made including mechanised locks. Whilst many of the locks vary in size the majority are - 85 ft long by 16 ft wide and between 5 and 7 feet deep. Upto Enfield Lock they are double locks and beyond to Hertford, single locks. The river can be either spelt Lee or Lea. The navigation forms part of a 50 mile Lea Valley walk from Limehouse Basin to Luton.

THE LEE VALLEY REGIONAL PARK - The first regional park in Britain, now covering 10,000 acres, along 26 miles of the River Lee (Lea). There are many picnic areas, car parks along its length, with excellent bus and rail links.

FINSBURY PARK, CROUCH END, PRIORY PARK, STATIONERS PARK, & RAILWAY FIELDS NATURE RESERVE - 6 MILES

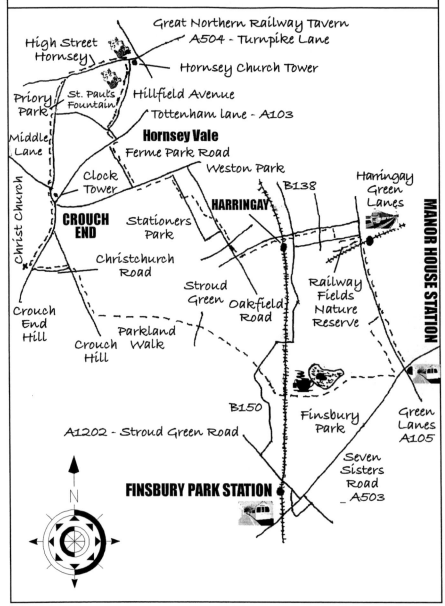

Great Northern Railway Tavern
A504 - Turnpike Lane
High Street Hornsey
Hornsey Church Tower
Priory Park
St. Paul's Fountain
Hillfield Avenue
Tottenham lane - A103
Middle Lane
Hornsey Vale
Ferme Park Road
Clock Tower
Weston Park
B138
Haringay Green Lanes
Christ Church
CROUCH END
Stationers Park
HARRINGAY
MANOR HOUSE STATION
Christchurch Road
Stroud Green
Oakfield Road
Railway Fields Nature Reserve
Crouch End Hill
Parkland Walk
Crouch Hill
B150
Finsbury Park
Green Lanes A105
A1202 - Stroud Green Road
N
FINSBURY PARK STATION
Seven Sisters Road - A503

FINSBURY PARK, CROUCH END, PRIORY PARK, STATIONERS PARK AND RAILWAY FIELDS NATURE RESERVE - 6 MILES - allow 3 hours.

Basic route - *Manor House Station - Finsbury Park - Parkland Walk - Crouch Hill - Crouch End - Clock Tower - Priory Park - Hornsey - Hornsey vale - Stationers Park - Railway Fields Nature Reserve - Manor House Station.*

Map - O.S. 1:25,000 Explorer series No. 173 - London North.

<u>*Start and end*</u> *- Manor House Underground Station (Piccadilly Line).*

Bus nos. 29, 253, 254, 259, 279.

Inns - Railway Tavern, King's Head, Crouch End. Hornsey Tavern, Three Compasses & the Great Northern Railway Tavern, Hornsey.

Cafe - Park Cafe, Finsbury Park. Several at Crouch End. Cafe in Priory Park.

ABOUT THE WALK - Finsbury Park is one of the largest and finest in London, and this walk takes you through it. Next you follow a section of the Parkland Walk & Capital Ring, before leaving it and ascending Crouch Hill and down to Crouch End and its magnificent Clock Tower. A short road walk brings you to the lesser known Priory Park with gardens and a fountain from St. Paul's cathedral gardens. Next you walk through Hornsey and just off the route is the medieval church tower. A road walk then leads to the surprise of the walk - Stationers Park. A small gem; a delightful park with fountains and a waterfall. Another road walk leads to your final "secret" place, The Railway Fields Nature Reserve - restricted entry times, see below - beside Harringay,

Green Lanes, Station. A few yards more and you are beside Finsbury Park and soon back at Manor House Station. A surprising walk full of interest and to some of the attractive and "hidden" places of central North London.

WALKING INSTRUCTIONS - From Manor House Station cross the main road and enter Finsbury Park. Keep straight ahead and cross the main driveway and keep to the lefthand path as you gently ascend and pass the "Lion" Monument to Helena Fedorowicz (1926-1993) on your left. Follow the path left through the McKenzie Gardens. Pass the children's play area, and now following the Capital Ring signs for the next 1 1/2 miles. Pass to your right the park's cafe and keep ahead to a railway footbridge. Cross and at the otherside turn right onto a path and the start of the Parkland Way; a former railway line to Alexandra Palace. Follow the path for more than a mile, crossing three road bridges and then under two more. After the second, by the sign Finsbury Park 1 mile, turn right onto a tarmaced path and ascend slightly to Crouch Hill road.

Turn left and ascend Crouch Hill and near the top pass a Haringey Borough boundary sign. Just after turn left along Christchurch Road to Crouch End Hill road and Christ Church opposite. Turn right down the hill passing Broadway Court and the Railway Tavern. Soon after pass the King's Head and the main shopping area of Crouch End - The Broadway. Pass the Town Hall on your right and onto the Clock Tower. Cross the road here and keep left along Park Road for a few strides before turning right, beside "Monkey Nuts", along Middle Lane. Follow the lane to the fourth road on your left - Chesnut Avenue and turn left into Priory Park. Cross the hard ball playing area and turn right into the gardens; before doing so just ahead is the paddling pool and park cafe. Walk through the gardens to St. Paul's Fountain. Continue ahead on the path to Hornsey High Street (A504) and turn right Immediacy passing the other end of Middle Lane.

Pass Hornsey Tavern and the Three Compasses before turning right along Hillfield Avenue. Before doing so just ahead is a former drinking fountain and water trough with the Great Northern Railway Tavern beyond. Opposite on the right is the churchyard and solitary medieval tower of the former Hornsey church. At the end of the avenue turn left to Tottenham Lane. To your left is Holy Innocents church and the Hornsey Historical Society Headquarters. (The building is the former school room of Holy Innocents School, built in 1848. The society have owned it since 1981). Cross and turn right and a few yards later left, along Ferme Park Road - road is signed for Stationers Park. Take the first road on your left - Weston Park, and then the third road on your right - Mayfield Road. Pass Hornsey Vale Centre and turn left into Stationers Park. Walk to the footbridge and water fountains and turn right to pass the waterfall and pond, before leaving the park and bear left past the children's play area to reach Denton Road.

Keep ahead now along Oakfield Road and take the second road on your left, Queensmore Road. At the end keep ahead across the railway bridge at Harringay Station to reach Wrightman Road. Go straight across along Burgoyne Road and at house no. 53, turn right through the passageway - Hornsey Passage - to Umfrevile Road. Turn left along this to Green Lanes (A105) and turn right to the Railway Fields Nature Reserve on the right with Green Lanes station just after. To return to Manor House Station, keep straight ahead along Green Lanes, soon passing Finsbury Park on your right. Little over 1/4 mile later regain Manor House Station on your left.

*Waterfall in
Stationers Park.*

CROUCH END CLOCK TOWER - The tower built in 1897 is in memory of Henry Reader Williams, a local man, who died 29th. September 1897. He was a wine merchant, a leading local Liberal politician and led a campaign to save Highgate Wood from development. He spent considerable time and effort and, "helped preserving local open spaces in Hornsey and Crouch End." This is one of the few monuments built before the honouree was dead, being unveiled on June 22nd. 1895.

ST. PAUL'S FOUNTAIN, PRIORY PARK - Was originally in St. Paul's churchyard in 1880 and made from Lamorna Granite, weighing 50 tons. In 1909 it was presented to the Borough of Hornsey by the City of London. Today, although the fountain is not working, the base, which has the City of London coat of arms on, makes a picturesque garden feature.

Priory Park was originally Pleasure Grounds laid out in 1894 by the Hornsey Urban District Council. In 1926 the grounds were extended with the purchase of Lewcock's Field and renamed Priory Park.

RAILWAY FIELDS NATURE RESERVE - Open Wednesday to Friday - 10 a.m. to 6 p.m.

Hornsey medieval church tower.

Hornsey drinking fountain and cattle water trough.

TWO WALKS FROM BOUNDS GREEN
- 2 AND 3 MILES

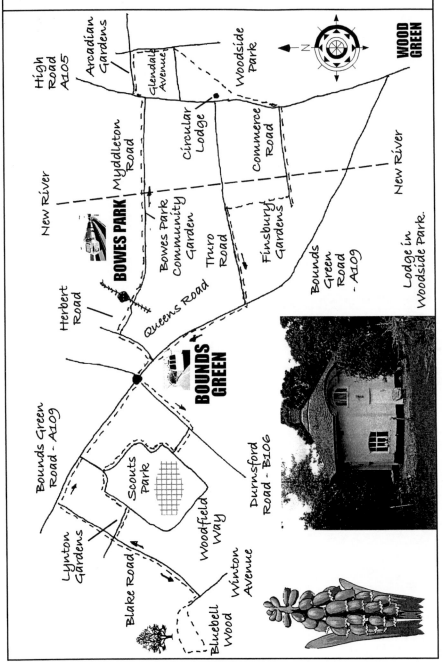

WOOD GREEN

High Road A105

Arcadian Gardens

Glendale Avenue

Woodside Park

Circular Lodge

Myddleton Road

Commerce Road

New River

New River

BOWES PARK

Bowes Park Community Garden

Truro Road

Finsbury Gardens

Bounds Green Road - A109

Lodge in Woodside Park.

Herbert Road

Queens Road

BOUNDS GREEN

Bounds Green Road - A109

Scouts Park

Durnsford Road - B106

Lynton Gardens

Blake Road

Woodfield Way

Winton Avenue

Bluebell Wood

TWO WALKS FROM BOUNDS GREEN - 2 AND 3 MILES - Allow 1 to 1 1/2 hours respectively.

 Start and end - **Bounds Green Underground Station (Piccadilly Line).**

 Bus nos. 184, 221, 299.

 Map - O. S. 1:25,000 Explorer Series No. 173 - London North.

BOUNDS GREEN - The underground station was built in 1932 and designed by Charles Holden. Originally the underground line was known as the London Electric Railway before becoming part of the Piccadilly Line. The name Bounds is believed to name after a family, Le Boundes, who are recorded to have lived here in the 13th. century. It is only in the last 100 years that the area has changed from a rural setting to suburbia.

WALK ONE - Scouts Park & Bluebell Wood - 2 miles - allow 1 hour.

ABOUT THE WALK - A short circular walk to the west of Bounds Green, to see a small attractive isolated wood - Bluebell Wood, beside Muswell Hill Golf Course. On the way you walk around the Scouts Park(Private) and return along the Bounds Green Road. This walk can be added to Walk 2 making a five mile altogether, as they form a figure of eight.

WALKING INSTRUCTIONS - Starting from the Bounds Green Underground Station, cross the main road - Bounds Green Road (A109) into Durnsford Road (B106). After 200 yards turn right into Woodfield Way. In a few yards turn right along Gordon Road, passing the entrance to the Scout Park. Just after turn left along Passmore Gardens, as you walk around the Scout Park. Turn left again into Woodfield Way and then the next right along

67

Lynton Gardens to Blake Road. Turn left and ascend slightly to junction of the road with Winton Avenue. Turn right - a no through road - and at the end enter Bluebell Wood. Keep ahead and follow the path around its perimeter, walking in an anticlockwise direction.

Returning to your entry point, turn right and retrace your steps along Winton Avenue and turn left along Blake Road. Follow this "downhill" to the Bounds Green Road. Turn right and follow it back to Bounds Green Underground Station.

WALK TWO - Bowes Park, Woodside Park and Hidden River Path - 3 miles - allow 1 1/2 hours.

 Cafe - Myddleton Cafe, Myddleton Road.

ABOUT THE WALK - A short circular walk on the east side of Bounds Green to the attractive Woodside Park. On the way you pass the small but important Bowes Park Community Garden and later walk along the Hidden River Path - New River. This walk can be added to Walk One, making an enjoyable 5 mile walk.

WALKING INSTRUCTIONS - From Bounds Green Underground Station, turn left along the main Bounds Green Road to where a footbridge crosses the road. Here turn left into Queens Road. Take the second road on your right - Herbert Road - and reach Bowes Park Station. Cross the footbridge into Ireland Place. Keep straight ahead across Whittington Russell Road into Myddleton Road - named after Sir Hugh Myddleton the creator of the New River, which you cross further along this road. Pass on the right the Bowes Park Community Garden and keep straight ahead to the A105 - High Road.

Cross and turn left and right to continue along Arcadian Gardens, passing the New Testament Church of God. Take the first road on the right - Glendale Avenue. At the second road on your right enter Woodside Park. Follow the tarmaced path diagonally across the park, noticing the unusual "circular" lodge on the right., to reach the High Road again. Turn left and pass Woodside House and soon afterwards cross and turn right along Commerce Road. At the end with Finsbury Road on the right, continue a few yards before turning right to walk along the Hidden River Path to Finsbury Gardens. Turn left along

Truro Road. At the end turn right along Trinity Road beside Bounds Green Road. Soon after join this road and keep ahead back to Bounds Green Underground Station.

WOODSIDE PARK LODGE - Built in 1822 and originally the gatehouse for Chitts House, which was demolished and now the site of Sylvan Road, just to the north. The "circular" building is one of Wood Green's oldest and most charming buildings.

MUSWELL HILL & COLDFALL WOOD
- 2 MILES

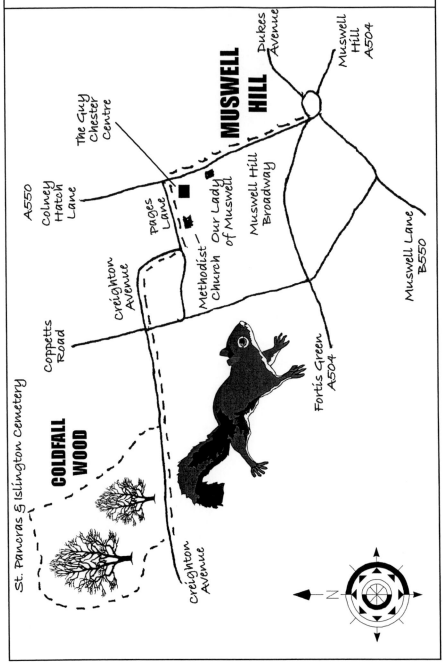

MUSWELL HILL

COLDFALL WOOD

Dukes Avenue

Muswell Hill A504

The Guy Chester Centre

Muswell Hill Broadway

A550 Colney Hatch Lane

Pages Lane

Our Lady of Muswell

Methodist Church

Creighton Avenue

Coppetts Road

Muswell Lane B550

Fortis Green A504

St. Pancras & Islington Cemetery

Creighton Avenue

N

MUSWELL HILL AND COLDFALL WOOD
- 2 MILES
- allow an hour or more.

Basic route - Muswell Hill - Broadway - Pages Lane - Creighton Avenue - Coldfall Wood - return same way.

O.S. MAP

Map - O.S. 1:25,000 Explorer Series No. 173 - London North.

<u>*Start and End -*</u> *Muswell Hill, Broadway - Bus Nos. W7, 144, 234, & 299.*

Inns and Cafe's - Several at Muswell Hill, shopping area.

ABOUT THE WALK - A short walk to one of Haringey's lesser known ancient woods. A short road walk through the cosmopolitan Muswell Hill brings you to the wood's entrance. You walk anticlockwise around the wood before retracing your steps back to Muswell Hill. The wood is a little hidden gem and well worth a trip to be back in unspoilt nature.

WALKING INSTRUCTIONS - Take the northern road from the central roundabout in Muswell Hill - Muswell Hill Broadway (A550). Pass shops and then Palace Mansions on the right and Our Lady of Muswell Hill, on the left. Soon after reach The Guy Chester Centre on the left and turn left along Pages Lane. Pass the Methodist church and turn right into Creighton Avenue. Follow the road round to your left and cross Coppetts Road, to continue along Creighton Avenue. Just after house no. 80, turn right into Coldfall Wood, at wood's sign and information board.

Follow the tarmaced path along the righthand side of the wood, with houses to your right. As you walk along the wood opens out on your left and you can see the stream and a wooden footbridge. Keep ahead to a seat on the right and the second wooden footbridge to your left - you are near the wood's end. Turn left and cross the footbridge and follow the path towards the wood's righthand corner, with the metal perimeter fence of the St. Pancras and Islington Cemetery ahead. Turn left on the path keeping near the wood's righthand side and follow this partially tarmaced path back to Creighton Avenue. Exiting the wood turn left and soon pass your entry point into the wood. Retrace your steps back to Muswell Hill. First cross Coppetts Road, and continue along Creighton Avenue to Pages Lane. Turn left to the A550 (Colney Hatch Road/Muswell Hill Broadway), beside the Guy Chester Centre. Turn right back along Muswell Broadway to central Muswell Hill and bus area.

COLDFALL WOOD - Predominantly oak trees upto 180 years old. other trees include holmbeam, hazel, holly, rowan and hawthorne. The wood is home to a variety of birds including jay, grey wagtail, green and spotted woodpeckers, tawny owl, wren and blackbirds. Woodland flowers include wood anemone, lady fern, dog violet and bluebells. A small stream runs through the wood which is crossed by two wooden bridges.

MUSWELL HILL - Whose name is derived from *"Mossy Well"*, has preserved its character because of its *"hill top"* location, and hence, no rail station; only accessible by bus. It is, therefore, a magnificent Edwardian Suburb. The well was believed to have medicinal qualities and King Malcolm I V (The Maiden) of Scotland,(died 1165) drank from the well and restored his health. The well known as a Holy Well and associated with the Virgin Mary, had associations with the nuns of St. Mary, Clerkenwell. A small chapel was built and for a while was a pilgrimage centre. In 1520 the well was recorded as one of the Marian shrines in the London area.

MUSWELL HILL ROAD JUNCTION - The five road junction - roundabout - at the top of Muswell Hill, was originally where the village pond was. Today it is hard to visualise a small village here surrounded by fields and countryside. In 1971 the pop group, The Kinks, released their album - *"Muswell Hillbillies."*

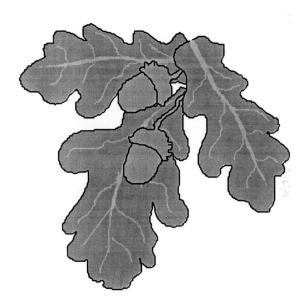

AROUND HARINGEY - 12 MILES

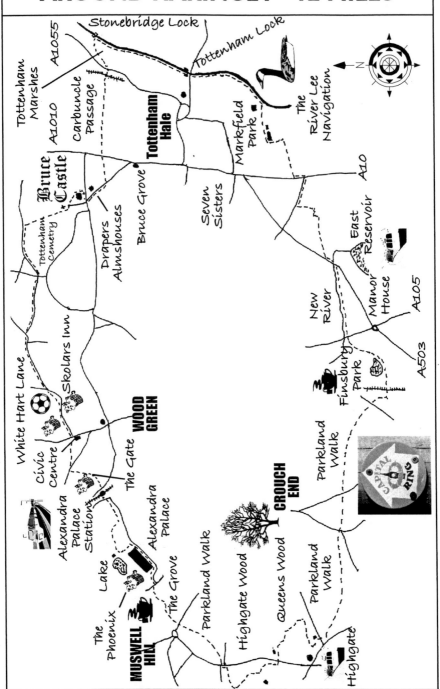

Basic route - Bruce Castle - Drapers Almshouses - Carbuncle Passage - Tottenham Marshes - Stonebridge Lock - River Lee Navigation - Tottenham Lock - Markfield Park - New River - Finsbury Park - Parkland Way - Capital Ring - Queens Wood - Highgate Wood - Parkland Walk - The Grove (Muswell Hill) - Alexandra Palace and Park - Haringey Civic Centre - White Hart Lane - Tottenham Cemetery and church - Bruce Castle.

O.S. MAP

Map - O.S. 1:25,000 Explorer Series No. 173 - North London.

<u>Start and end</u> - Bruce Castle. Bus nos. 123, 318, Nearest rail station - Bruce Grove.
The walk can be joined or left at the following stations, which are passed on the route/close to, in walking order - Tottenham Hale, Manor House, Highgate, and Alexandra Palace.

Inns - Victoria Free House, Scotland Green. The Golden Stool, A10 High Road. The Phoenix Inn, Alexandra Palace. The Gate Inn, opposite Alexandra Palace Station. The Prince Inn, Bounds Green Road. Skolars Inn, White Hart Lane.

Cafe - Stonebridge Lock. Finsbury Park. Queens Wood. Highgate Wood. Alexandra Palace - The Grove and beside the boating lake.

ABOUT THE WALK - The route is basically the one devised by Haringey Council - Better Haringey Trail Guide, with a few alternative paths. The walk encircles the borough and is almost a boundary walk. By doing the circuit you come to many of the features and scenic paths and parks that make up the borough. You also walk a section of the River Lee Navigation, the New River and Capital Ring. Intermingled are a wide variety of wildlife, woodland, views to the London skyline and a wealth of history. It is very much a grand slam of the borough and will no doubt encourage you to explore more fully several areas, which are in enumerated as separate walks in this book. So set off and see for yourself the surprising diversity of the borough.

Bruce Castle.

WALKING INSTRUCTIONS - Starting from the entrance gates to Bruce Castle - you walk through the park and can visit the castle's museum, at the end. Cross the road and turn half left down Bruce Grove - Bruce Grove Station is at the end of this road. Almost immediately pass the Drapers Almshouses - built in 1870. Turn left at the first road on your left - Hartham Road. Follow it right and at the bottom reach Newlyn Road. Turn left and right to continue along Pembury Road. Pass under the railway line and reach Tottenham High Road (A1010). Cross and reach Scotland Green. Pass the Victoria Free House and pleasant 19th. century cottages. Keep ahead and soon follow the path on the right of Hartington Park. At the end reach Hollington Road. Go straight across into the wide Carbuncle Passage, passing gardens and garages. At the end go straight across Shelbourne Road to reach a foot bridge over the railway and Watermead Way (A1055) and gain Tottenham Marshes.

River Lee Navigation ner Stonebridge Lock.

Follow the gravel path on the left to the car park and Stonebridge Lock (cafe) and the River Lee Navigation. Turn right and walk along the towpath for the next 1 1/2 miles. In more than 1/2 mile reach Tottenham Lock. Continue beside the navigation and pass under the road bridge - Ferry lane (A503). Follow the towpath as it curves right and pass under two rail bridges, as the navigation becomes a popular rowing area. Soon after the second bridge leave the towpath and turn right into Markfield Park. Keep straight ahead on the main path. In a short distance on your right is the Markfield Beam Engine (Museum). Keep ahead and pass the Rose Garden and reach Crowland Road. Continue ahead passing Gladesmore Community School and Crowland School. Just after turn left into Elm Park Avenue. Take the third road on your right - Gladesmore Road - and follow it to its end and junction with the A10 High Road. To your right is The Golden Stool Inn. Cross to your left to continue along St. Ann's Road with the church on the corner. Near the Plevna and Triangle Children's Centre, turn left along Eastbourne Road. Partway along bear right across Paignton Road Open Space to Richmond Road, Turn left along it. At the top turn right along Varty Road, and pass the attractive "Aged Pilgrims Friends Society", Almshouses - 1883 - on your right. Follow the road to Seven Sisters Road (A503).

Cross the road and either walk along Eade Road with the New River up the bank on the left - at the end turn left along Hermitage Road. Alternatively, after crossing the road turn left and then right to walk beside the New River. Both routes meet at Green Lane - A105 - with Manor House Underground station to your left. Cross the road and enter Finsbury Park, now on the

77

The Aged Pilgrims Friend Societys Home - 1883.

Capital Ring walk, which you follow for the next three miles - the Big Ben logo acts as your guide. Keep straight ahead - the New River turns right - and ascend first to a shelter and then through the Mackenzie Gardens and on past the lake, play area and cafe. Continue ahead and follow the path down to a bridge over the railway line. Immediately across, turn right onto the Parkland Walk - former railway line to Alexandra Palace.

Keep to the former railway line for the next two miles passing under road bridges and Crouch End and past a former station. Approaching a tunnel, follow the path left upto the road - path signed Muswell Hill 3 miles - to Holmesdale Road. Turn right and ascend to the main road with Highgate Station near by. Turn right into Shepherds Hill passing the tube station entrance on your left. In a few yards reach the Library and turn left and descend to Priory Gardens. Turn right and where the road ascends turn left, as signed into Queens Wood. Guided by Capital Ring Posts descend and ascend to Queens Wood Road. Cross back into Queens Wood. Keep straight ahead guided by Capital Ring posts, as you ascend and curve left then right to descend again before ascending to pass the cafe and reach Muswell Hill Road.

Cross the road to New Gate and follow the righthand path. At the next junction turn left, following the path signs - Cafe. You can keep to the righthand path

78

The Promenade, Alexandra Palace.

and follow it to Cranley Gardens where you rejoin the Parkland Walk. At the next junction and sign, the cafe is to your left. Turn right and at the next junction with a former water fountain just ahead, turn left along the wide path, still on the Capital Ring, to the Bridge Gate entrance to Highgate Wood. Immediately before it turn right along the path and descend gradually to Cranley Gate. Turn left and in a few yards keep left to descend and regain the former railway line. Turn right along it passing under a road bridge. Soon the path goes along a railway viaduct which is an exceptional vantage point over a large area of London, although you can't see its skyline, yet. Later pass through a small tunnel at Muswell Hill and reach The Grove and Alexandra Park.

Follow the path through the bridges and entering The Grove keep to the lefthand path and pass the cafe. Afterwards reach the car park. Walk through to the road and bear left and ascend to Alexandra Palace, the Phoenix Inn and Palm Court entrance. Walk around the righthand side of the building, along The Promenade, to get the views over the London's skyline. At the end of the building turn left through the car park to the lake (cafe). Keep right on the path to pass the deer enclosure and follow the "drive" round to your right. Before the Alexandra Palace Way, turn left on the tarmaced path and descend paralleling the road to the park's entrance. Turn left and right to walk across the footbridge over the railway line to Alexandra Palace Station.

Obelisk and fountain,
opposite The Prince Inn,
Bounds Green Road.
In memory of Catherine Smithies,
Founder of the Band of Mercy
Movement.

Cross Buckingham Road and walk along the righthand side of The Gate Inn along St. Michael's Terrace. At the end keep ahead in an open space and now rejoined the New River Path, as you follow the central path to Bounds Green Road with an obelisk fountain and The Prince Inn opposite. Cross the road and reach Trinity Road. Turn right along it passing the Greek Orthodox Cathedral on your left. At the end on your right is Haringey Civic Centre, built on the site of two almshouses. Cross the road into White Hart Lane. Follow it past the Woodside Day Centre and just after you can walk across the Lane Recreation Ground, thus cutting the road corner off. On the road is the Skolars Inn. Regaining the road, near Wolves Road, keep right, still along White Hart Lane. Pass on the left the White Hart Lane Community Sports Centre. Soon after at St. George's Industrial Estate, turn right into Rivulet Road. Follow this to its end and gain the Great Cambridge Road (A10).

Turn left to cross the road via the footbridge. Over, turn left and then right to continue along White Hart Lane. Soon reach Tottenham Cemetery on your right. Continue a little further to a path sign and turn right along the fenced Church Path passing the cemetery and onto Tottenham Church. Continue past it on your left to the road - Church Lane. On the right is the Priory with attractive wrought iron gates. Cross into Bruce's Castle Park and keep right along the path back to the Museum and where you began a few hours ago.

CARBUNCLE PASSAGE - Beneath the surface runs the Moselle River and this section was known as Garbell Ditch.

TOTTENHAM MARSHES - Once Haringey's airfield where John A. Prestwich flew his JAP monoplane on April 10th. 1910. The plane is now on display in the Science Museum. The Marshes were part of the robbers route in the Tottenham Outrage - see separate walk for details. The Marshes are also part of the Lee Valley Regional Park.

MARKFIELD PARK - As the name implies the fields marks the onetime boundary between Tottenham and Hackney.

NEW RIVER - see separate walk for history notes.

FINSBURY PARK - Covers 115 acres and was opened in 1869 it is one of the largest and oldest parks in Haringey. In 2006 a multimillion pound lottery grant enabled the park to be fully restored.

PARKLAND WALK - *"The Muswell Hill and Palace Railway"*. Former railway line to Alexandra Palace, opened on Monday 2nd. June 1873, when 60,000 people visited the Palace. 16 days later it burnt down and the train ceased. The Palace was rebuilt in 1874 and the train line reopened. Near Muswell Hill the line crosses St. James Lane by a 17 brick arched viaduct.

QUEENS WOOD - Formerly known as Church Bottom Wood was renamed Queens Wood in 1898, after Queen Victoria. Together with Highgate Wood they formed part of the Great Forest of Middlesex.

HIGHGATE WOOD - Formerly known as Brew House Wood.

THE GROVE - Part of a former estate added to Alexandra Palace in 1863. The house was demolished in 1873 with the building of the railway line to the Palace.

HARINGEY CIVIC CENTRE, WOOD GREEN - Stands on the site of the Fishmongers and Poulters Almshouses. Designed by Sir John Brown and built between 1955-8.

Fancy a challenge?

Why not walk the North London - Three Borough Challenge Walk - 21 miles

linking together the three borough's of Enfield, Barnet and Haringey. You can walk it in stages!

NORTH LONDON THREE BOROUGH CHALLENGE WALK - ENFIELD, BARNET & HARINGEY

Statue of Peace, Friary Park.

Highgate Wood.

New River in Haringey.

by John N. Merrill

WALTHAMSTOW TO WOOD GREEN
- 8 MILES

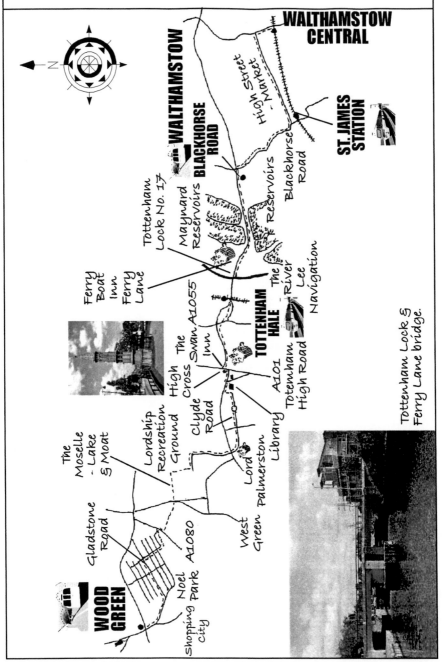

WALTHAMSTOW CENTRAL

WALTHAMSTOW

High Street - Market

ST. JAMES STATION

BLACKHORSE ROAD

Blackhorse Road

Reservoirs

Tottenham Lock No. 17

Maynard Reservoirs

Ferry Boat Inn Ferry Lane

The River Lee Navigation

Swan A1055

TOTTENHAM HALE

The High Cross Inn

High Cross Road

A101 Tottenham High Road

Clyde Road

Library

Lordship Recreation Ground

Lord Palmerston

West Green

The Moselle - Lake & Moat

Gladstone Road

Noel Park A1080

Shopping City

WOOD GREEN

Tottenham Lock & Ferry Lane bridge.

A Town to Town Walk - WALTHAMSTOW TO WOOD GREEN - 8 MILES - allow 3 to 4 hours.

Basic route - Walthamstow Central Station - High Street Market - Blackhorse Road - Stoneytown Park - Blackhorse Station - Ferry Lane - Ferry Boat Inn - The Paddock Community Nature Park - Tottenham Hale Station - High Cross, Tottenham - Tottenham Green Library - Clyde Road - Lordship Recreation Ground - Noel Park - Noel Park - Wood Green Station.

Map - O.S. 1:25,000 Explorer Series No. 173 - London North.

<u>Start -</u> Walthamstow Central Station - Bus and Underground (Victoria Line).

Bus nos. 20, 34, 48, 58, 215, 257, W11.
<u>End -</u> Wood Street Underground Station (Piccadilly Line). Bus. nos. 29, 67, 123, 230.

On the way you pass Blackhorse Road Underground Station (Victoria Line) and Tottenham Hale Underground (Victoria Line), rail and bus station.

Inns - Ferry Boat Inn, Ferry Lane. The Swan Inn, Tottenham High Cross. The Lord Palmerston, Philip Lane. Wood Green.

Cafe - Several along High Street (Walthamstow Market). Tottenham Hale. Wood Green.

ABOUT THE WALK - The basic aim of the walk is to link "towns" together, making an alternative to overland transport, to get some exercise and see some of historic buildings and parks along the way. The first part is in the borough of Waltham Forest, as you walk through one of the biggest outdoor markets in England - a mile long, along Walthamstow High Street - so you can shop as you walk! Road walking brings you to Blackhorse Road and Station, before walking between the reservoirs and across the River Lee Navigation and into the Borough of Haringey. You pass Tottenham Hale Station before a short historical walk as you pass Tottenham High Cross, well, church and Sunday School. Using quiet roads you reach Lordship Recreation Ground, and walk beside The Moselle and lake. Soon after, you reach Noel Park and the final section past the houses of Noel Park to Wood Green. To the left is Shopping City and more shopping opportunities!

WALKING INSTRUCTIONS - Starting from Walthamstow Central Underground and bus Station, cross the road and cross the open space, passing the entrance to Selbourne Walk Shopping Mall on the left and Walthamstow Library on the right. Just after reach Walthamstow High Street and market. Turn left and for nearly a mile walk through the market. After almost 1/2 mile cross Palmerston Road, and keep ahead still through the market area to the main road - Blackhorse Road. To your left is St. James Station. Turn right along the road and pass Our Lady of Rosary and St. Patrick, then the Baptist Church. Next, pass St. Mary's Terrace and on the right is Stoneytown Park. Soon after reach Blackhorse Underground Station on the left and junction with Forest Road (A503).

Cross the road and turn left along it. Soon pass the High and Low Maynard Reservoirs on the right and Reservoirs No. 2 and 4 on the left. Keep ahead along the road, which now becomes Ferry Lane. Pass the Ferry Boat Inn and step into Haringey Borough. Pass the Paddock Community Nature Park on the right - well worth a side walk, returning back to the road. Just after cross the bridge over the River Lee Navigation - *opened on March 30th. 1918 and replacing the earlier bridge of 1760*. Pass Tottenham Lock No. 17 on the right. Not long after is Tottenham Hale Station on the right and a retail Park on the left.

Keep straight ahead and cross three roads via crossings to The Hale road. Turn left and immediately right, as cycled path signed, along the path into High Cross Road. Follow it right and left towards a school and Imani House on the right. Turn right here, along the path to Monument Way and turn left to its junction with Tottenham High Road, with the High Cross on the right, and the Swan Inn and Tottenham Green Well opposite. Cross the road to near the well and turn right and left to continue along Philip Lane. Pass the Town Hall Approach Road on the left, and then the Tottenham Green Library and Leisure centre on the left, as the road curves right.

Immediately after turn left along Clyde Road and at the end turn right, still on Clyde Road, and cross the railway bridge. Keep straight ahead to Clyde Circus roundabout and continue ahead, still on Clyde Road and reach Lawrence Road. Go straight across and pass Elizabeth Place Play Area. The road curves right to the Lord Palmerston public house and Philip Lane. Go straight across and pass St. Philip church on the corner, as you walk along Conmell Road. At the end turn left along Higham Road. Opposite house no. 99 turn right into the Lordship Recreation Ground. Keep ahead along the path towards a hedge and turn left onto another path that leads around the lake - Homestead Pond and former Angle Saxon Moat. Pass a pool and children's play area and gain Downhills Way.

Go straight across into Sandringham Road and at the end turn right along Rusper Road to the main road - A1080 - Westbury Avenue. Cross and turn right and follow it for more 100 yards to the entrance to Noel Park on the left. Follow the tarmaced path and at the play area turn right to exit the park and reach Darwin Road. Keep ahead along here and take the fourth road on your left - Gladstone Road - you are now in the housing estate of Noel Park. Keep along this avenue which later curves right with St. Mark's church on the left. At the end reach The Broadway - Wood Green High Road. Turn right and in a few strides you are at Wood Green Station; whilst to your left is Shopping City.

THE FERRY BOAT INN - Formerly three buildings of the 17th/18th century and the original ferry house, before the road bridge was built.

NOEL PARK ESTATE - Covers 100 acres and was originally built as low rent houses by the Artisans, Labourers and General Dwellings Company. They bought the land in 1881 and Rowland Plumbe designed the layout. Work began in 1883 and by 1907 it was basically complete.

WALK RECORD PAGE

The Capital Ring in Haringey - 4 1/2 miles ....

The New River in Haringey - 4 1/2 miles ....

East Finchley Circular walk -
includes the Haringey sections of the Capital Ring and New River
plus a walk through Alexandra Park - 12 miles ....

Alexandra Palace and Park - 3 miles ....

Tottenham High Road - a historical walk - 1 1/2 miles ....

Six Parks of Tottenham - 7 miles ....

.

Tottenham Marshes - 4 miles ....

Finsbury Park, Crouch End, Priory Park, Stationers Park
and Railway Fields Nature Reserve - 6 miles ....

Two walks from Bounds Green - 2 and 3 miles ....

Muswell Hill & Coldfall Wood - 2 miles ....

Around Haringey (Boundary walk) - 12 miles ....

A Town to Town Walk - Walthamstow to Wood Green - 8 miles ....

THE JOHN MERRILL WALK BADGE

Complete six walks in this book and get the above special embroidered
badge and signed certificate. Badges are Black cloth
with lettering and hiker embroidered in four colours.

BADGE ORDER FORM

Date walks completed...

NAME ....

ADDRESS ....

....

Price: £5.00 each including postage, packing, VAT and signed completion
certificate. Amount enclosed (Payable to The John Merrill Foundation).

Happy Walking T Shirt - yellow - £8.95 inc. postage - state size required.

From: The John Merrill Foundation,
32, Holmesdale, Waltham Cross,
Hertsfordshire, EN8 8QY

Tel/Fax 01992 - 762776
e-mail - marathonhiker@aol.com

Order on line - www.johnmerrillwalkguides.com

********* YOU MAY PHOTOCOPY THIS FORM **********

THE LONDON BOROUGHS WALKS SERIES

Each book explores all the walks within the boundaries of the borough, including sections of the recreational paths - The Capital Ring and London Loop. Also all waymarked paths in each borough and along any canal or navigation. Paths/ routes linking parks together are also written about. Plus details of shorter walks in Open Spaces and Nature Reserves. Each book attempts to cover all the walks in each borough, together with considerable local history, adding interest and purpose to each walk. Details of how to get to a walks' start by bus, underground and train is included, together with details of what Ordnance Survey map is needed, plus inns and cafe's along the way. Combined, all you need to explore a given area of London. London has much to offer the walker and explorer and it is hope these walks will prove an eye-opener to the historic countryside on your doorstep.

....*Happy walking!*

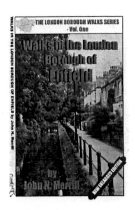

Vol. One - WALKS IN THE LONDON BOROUGH OF ENFIELD

The London Borough of Enfield, is London's most northern borough, with some 40 miles of footpaths. Passing through the area are the signed paths of the London Loop, River Lee Navigation, Pymmes Brook Trail and the New River. They provide rewarding countryside walking, but the borough has much more to offer. With some delightful town parks and country parks. Added to this are some fascinating buildings, in Enfield and Edmonton, and a rich history, providing enjoyable walks in both town and countryside.

Here are twleve walks and a 25 miles challenge walk, which explore the Borough fully; whether you are a local or not, the walks will come as a pleasant surprise in the surrounding suburbia.

New Enlarged Edition.

A5 wire bound. 104 pages. 16 maps. 43 photographs.   £9.95

ISBN 978-0-9556511-2-0

Vol. Two - WALKS IN THE LONDON BOROUGH OF BARNET

Includes historical walks in Barnet and around the Battle of Barnet area. The Dollis Valley Green Walk, the Pymmes Brook Trail, The London Loop and Capital Ring sections in the borough. Plus walks around Totteridge and Mill Hill, Edgware and many of the parks, including Sunnyhill, Brunswick Park, Oak Hill Park and Stoneyfields Park. 15 walks plus suggestions for other short walks. Combined they encompass the whole of the borough.

A5. 124 Pages. 18 maps. 43 photographs. Wire Bound. £9.95
ISBN 978-0-9556511-4-4

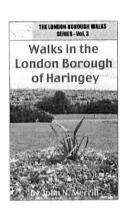

Vol. Three - WALKS IN THE LONDON BOROUGH OF HARINGEY

12 walks, includes historical walks inTottenham High Road, Park walks, the New River, Capital Ring and River Lee Navigation - Tottenham Marshes - the scene of the Tottenham Outrage. Other walks explore the parks of Tottenham, Muswell Hill, Crouch End, Hornsey and to some of the stunning hidden places - parks and woods - of the borough. Alexandra Palace and Park, has its own walk around this amazing place. One 12 mile walk totally encircles the borough.

100 pages. 40 photographs. 14 maps.
A5. Wire bound. £9.95.
ISBN 978-0-9556511-8-2

Vol. Four - WALKS IN THE LONDON BOROUGH OF WALTHAM FOREST

Includes historical walks in Chingford, Leyton and Walthamstow, the River Lee Navigation and Epping Forest. A 24 mile boundary walk, a walk around Walthamstow Village, and walks in conservation areas and parks. 15 walks altogether.

120 pages. 18 maps. 65 photographs. A5. Wire bound.

91

OTHER NORTH LONDON WALK BOOKS
by JOHN N. MERRILL

SHORT CIRCULAR WALKS ON THE RIVER LEE NAVIGATION - Northern Volume - Ponder's End - Hertford. 64 pages, 23 photographs, 10 detailed maps and walks. History notes. - ISBN 1-903627-68-0 @ £6.95 **WALKING THE RIVER LEE NAVIGATION - VOL 1 & 2.**

SHORT CIRCULAR WALKS ON THE NEW RIVER & SOUTH EAST HERTFORDSHIRE 11 walks - 5 to 10 miles long between Waltham Cross and Hertford; many on the New River. New revised and enlarged edition 68 pages, 24 photographs, 13 detailed maps. History notes. ISBN 1-903627-69-9 @ £6.95

SHORT CIRCULAR WALKS IN EPPING FOREST 10 circular walks 6 to 18 miles long. Combined they explore the whole forest and its surrounding area. 68 pages. 12 maps. 30 photographs. History notes. ISBN 1-903627-72-9 @ £6.95

LONG CIRCULAR WALKS IN EASTERN HERTFORDSHIRE 9 walks - 15 to 20 miles long. Beautiful unspoilt walking in rolling countryside full of historical interest. ISBN 978-0-9553691-7-9

LONG CIRCULAR WALKS IN WESTERN HERTFORDSHIRE - 9 long walks - 15 to 20 miles.. 112 pages. Wire bound. 55 photographs. 20 detailed maps. £9.95 ISBN 978-0-955651113

SHORT CIRCULAR WALKS ON THE RIVER STORT NAVIGATION 8 circular walks; 1 End to End walk. Full history and photographic study of this peaceful waterway. 92 pages. 68 photographgs. 12 maps. ISBN 1-903627- 73-7 £8.95

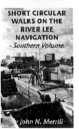

SHORT CIRCULAR WALKS ON THE RIVER LEE NAVIGATION - Southern Volume - Limehouse basin to Hackney Marsh. 5 walks on the Regent Canal, Hertford Union and Limehouse Cut. Including Three Mills and its rivers. The guide also details a 28 mile End to End walk along the Navigation. 68 pages. 10 maps, 30 photographs. ISBn 1-903627-74-5 £6.95

EPPING FOREST CHALLENGE WALK - 21 MILES. Starts and ends at Waltham Abbey and takes in the whole forest. 44 pages. 6 maps. 10 photos £5.95 ISBN 978-0-9553691-0-0

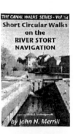

"St. ALBANS WAY" - 26 mile Pilgrims walk from Waltham Abbey to St. Alban's Cathedral. £5.95 ISBN 978-0-9553691-3-1

WALKS IN THE LONDON BOROUGH OF ENFIELD 12 walks throughout the borough. 18 maps. 54 photos. 106 pages. ISBN 978-0955651120 £9.95

WALKS IN THE LONDON OF BARNET
WALKS IN THE LONDON BOROUGH OF HARINGEY
WALKS IN THE LONDON BOROUGH OF WALTHAM FOREST

OTHER LONDON CANAL WALK BOOKS
by JOHN N. MERRILL

SHORT CIRCULAR WALKS ON THE RIVER LEE NAVIGA-TION - Northern Volume - Ponder's End - Hertford.
60 pages, 23 photographs, 10 detailed maps and walks. History notes.
- ISBN 1-903627-68-0 @ £6.95

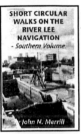

SHORT CIRCULAR WALKS ON THE RIVER LEE NAVIGA-TION - Southern Volume - Limehouse basin to Hackney Marsh.
5 walks on the Regent Canal, Hertford Union and Limehouse Cut.
Including Three Mills and its rivers. The guide also details a 28 mile
End to End walk along the Navigation.
68 pages. 10 maps, 30 photographs.
ISBn 1-903627-74-5
£6.95

**SHORT CIRCULAR WALKS ON THE RIVER STORT
NAVIGATION**
8 circular walks; 1 End to End walk. Full history and photographic
study of this peaceful waterway. 92 pages. 68 photographgs. 12 maps.
ISBN 1-903627- 73-7 £8.95

**SHORT CIRCULAR WALKS ON THE NEW RIVER &
SOUTH EAST HERTFORDSHIRE**
11 walks - 5 to 10 miles long between Waltham Cross and Hertford;
many on the New River. New revised and enlarged edition 68 pages,
24 photographs , 13 detailed maps. History notes.
ISBN 1-903627-69-9 @ £6.95

"WALKING LONDON'S CANALS -
Regent's Canal, River Thames, Isle of Dogs and Grand Union Canal.
10 walks. 108 pages. 85 photos. Wire bound. 14 detailed maps. £9.95
ISBN 978-0-9553691-2-4

"WALKING THE STREETS OF LONDON -
7 - Historical short walks in the city. 112 pages. Wire bound. 96
photographs. 12 detailed maps.
£9.95 ISBN 978-0-9553691-1-7

THE AIM OF THE BOOK

The aim of this book was simply to walk every waymarked path within the confines of London and it's borough's and within the M25. There are a surprising number of routes, as this book demonstrates; combined there are some 600 miles of walking.

All the walks in this book can be done at your own pace; you don't have to walk the whole individual walk in a day. You can do in stages for there is always much to see and admire on the way. At the back of the book is a walk log so you can record when you walked each route.

The last walk in the book is my own creation - A walk for peace - and is a walk for quiet contemplation, while visiting three unique Buddhist sites.

ISBN978-0-9556511-3-7   £12.95   184 pages. 50 maps, 30 b/w photos.

OTHER JOHN MERRILL WALK BOOKS

For a free complete catalogue of John Merrill walk Guides send a SAE to The John Merrill Foundation

*Visit our website -
www.johnmerrillwalkguides.com*

THE LITTLE JOHN CHALLENGE WALK
YORKSHIRE DALES CHALLENGE WALK
NORTH YORKSHIRE MOORS CHALLENGE WALK
LAKELAND CHALLENGE WALK
THE RUTLAND WATER CHALLENGE WALK
MALVERN HILLS CHALLENGE WALK
THE SALTER'S WAY
THE SNOWDON CHALLENGE
CHARNWOOD FOREST CHALLENGE WALK
THREE COUNTIES CHALLENGE WALK (Peak District).
CAL-DER-WENT WALK by Geoffrey Carr,
THE QUANTOCK WAY
BELVOIR WITCHES CHALLENGE WALK
THE CARNEDDAU CHALLENGE WALK
THE SWEET PEA CHALLENGE WALK
THE LINCOLNSHIRE WOLDS - BLACK DEATH - CHALLENGE WALK
JENNIFER'S CHALLENGE WALK
THE EPPING FOREST CHALLENGE WALK

INSTRUCTION & RECORD -
HIKE TO BE FIT.....STROLLING WITH JOHN
THE JOHN MERRILL WALK RECORD BOOK
HIKE THE WORLD - John Merrill's guide to walking & Backpacking.

MULTIPLE DAY WALKS -
THE RIVERS'S WAY
PEAK DISTRICT: HIGH LEVEL ROUTE
PEAK DISTRICT MARATHONS
THE LIMEY WAY
THE PEAKLAND WAY
COMPO'S WAY by Alan Hiley
THE BRIGHTON WAY by Norman Willis

THE PILGRIM WALKS SERIES -
THE WALSINGHAM WAY - Ely to Walsingham - 72 miles
THE WALSINGHAM WAY - Kings Lynn to Walsingham - 35 miles
TURN LEFT AT GRANJA DE LA MORERUELA - 700 miles
NORTH TO SANTIAGO DE COMPOSTELA, VIA FATIMA - 650 miles
St. OLAV'S WAY - Oslo to Trondheim - 400 miles
St. WINEFRIDE'S WAY - St. Asaph to Holywell
St. ALBANS WAY - Waltham Abbey to St. Albans - 26 miles
St. KENELM TRAIL by John Price - Clent Hills to Winchcombe - 60 miles
DERBYSHIRE PILGRIMAGES

COAST WALKS & NATIONAL TRAILS -
ISLE OF WIGHT COAST PATH
PEMBROKESHIRE COAST PATH
THE CLEVELAND WAY
WALKING ANGELSEY'S COASTLINE.
WALKING THE COASTLINE OF THE CHANNEL ISLANDS
THE ISLE OF MAN COASTAL PATH - "The Way of the Gull."
A WALK AROUND HAYLING ISLAND
A WALK AROUND THE ISLE OF SHEPPEY

DERBYSHIRE & PEAK DISTRICT HISTORICAL GUIDES -
A to Z GUIDE OF THE PEAK DISTRICT
DERBYSHIRE INNS - an A to Z guide
HALLS AND CASTLES OF THE PEAK DISTRICT & DERBYSHIRE
TOURING THE PEAK DISTRICT & DERBYSHIRE BY CAR
DERBYSHIRE FOLKLORE
PUNISHMENT IN DERBYSHIRE
CUSTOMS OF THE PEAK DISTRICT & DERBYSHIRE
WINSTER - A SOUVENIR GUIDE
ARKWRIGHT OF CROMFORD
LEGENDS OF DERBYSHIRE
DERBYSHIRE FACTS & RECORDS
TALES FROM THE MINES by Geoffrey Carr
PEAK DISTRICT PLACE NAMES by Martin Spray
DERBYSHIRE THROUGH THE AGES - Vol 1 -DERBYSHIRE IN PREHISTORIC TIMES
SIR JOSEPH PAXTON
FLORENCE NIGHTINGALE
JOHN SMEDLEY
BONNIE PRINCE CHARLIE & 20 mile walk.
THE STORY OF THE EARLS AND DUKES OF DEVONSHIRE

For a free
complete
catalogue of
John Merrill
walk Guides
send a SAE to
The John Merrill
Foundation

JOHN MERRILL'S MAJOR WALKS -
TURN RIGHT AT LAND'S END
WITH MUSTARD ON MY BACK
TURN RIGHT AT DEATH VALLEY
EMERALD COAST WALK
I CHOSE TO WALK - Why I walk etc.
A WALK IN OHIO - 1,310 miles around the Buckeye Trail.

Visit our website -
www.johnmerrillwalkguides.com

SKETCH BOOKS -
SKETCHES OF THE PEAK DISTRICT

COLOUR BOOK:-
THE PEAK DISTRICT.......something to remember her by.

OVERSEAS GUIDES -
HIKING IN NEW MEXICO - Vol I - The Sandia and Manzano Mountains.
Vol 2 - Hiking "Billy the Kid" Country. Vol 4 - N.W. area - " Hiking Indian Country."
"WALKING IN DRACULA COUNTRY" - Romania.
WALKING THE TRAILS OF THE HONG KONG ISLANDS.

VISITOR GUIDES - MATLOCK . BAKEWELL. ASHBOURNE.